Helen R Cutler

Jottings from Life

Or, Passages from the Diary of an Itinerant's Wife

Helen R Cutler

Jottings from Life

Or, Passages from the Diary of an Itinerant's Wife

ISBN/EAN: 9783337019952

Printed in Europe, USA, Canada, Australia, Japan

Cover: Foto ©ninafisch / pixelio.de

More available books at **www.hansebooks.com**

JOTTINGS FROM LIFE;

OR,

PASSAGES FROM THE DIARY OF AN ITINERANT'S WIFE.

BY

HELEN R. CUTLER.

CINCINNATI:
PUBLISHED BY POE & HITCHCOCK.
R. P. THOMPSON, PRINTER.
1866.

Entered, according to Act of Congress, in the year 1864,

BY POE & HITCHCOCK,

In the Clerk's Office of the District Court for the Southern District of Ohio.

CONTENTS.

CHAPTER I.

TILL I ENTERED THE MINISTRY.

	PAGE.
1. Parents and Early Life	11
2. Choice among Wooers	13
3. Home-leaving	16

CHAPTER II.

OUR FIRST CIRCUIT.

1. Farmer Griffith	18
2. Self-Communings	23
3. The Next Morning	28
4. The Parsonage	31
5. The Village	34
6. New Resolutions; or, Old Habits	35

CHAPTER III.

SUNDAY JOTTINGS TO FILL OUT.

1. Frank's Cousin	38
2. Widow Barker	39

CONTENTS.

	PAGE.
3. Self-Improvement	42
4. Growing Tolerant	43
5. Pleasant Memories	44
6. Sarah Griffith	46
7. Methodism One Every-where	48

CHAPTER IV.

OUR SECOND CIRCUIT.

1. A Bird's-eye View ... 50
2. Making One's Self Agreeable ... 53
3. Literary Gleanings ... 55
4. In Heaviness of Spirit ... 57
5. Uses of Censorious Persons ... 60
6. Timely Gift ... 64

CHAPTER V.

JOTTINGS IN CONTINUANCE.

1. Widow Barker in a new Character ... 68
2. Father Braden ... 72
3. Letter from Sarah Griffith ... 75
4. Conquering Self ... 77
5. Chitchat about Female Authors ... 79
6. A Talk about the Itinerancy ... 80
7. Sabbath Evening Thoughts ... 84
8. The Minister's Wife at a Party ... 86

CONTENTS.

CHAPTER VI.

AT ANOTHER POST.

		PAGE.
1.	Making and Parting from Friends	94
2.	Henry again with us	95
3.	Little Acts and Great Principles	97
4.	"Did n't Think," no Excuse for Neglect of Duty.	99
5.	Our Donation Party	102

CHAPTER VII.

PERSONS, OPINIONS, AND CRITICISMS.

1.	Morrison; or, both Kinds of Laziness	109
2.	Shall I take Lessons in Music and French?	115
3.	Allston; or, the Selfish Student	119
4.	Caught in a Bad Plight	121
5.	Brockway; or, the Downward Career	124
6.	Soon to be on the Wing Again	129
7.	Moral Law a Reality	132

CHAPTER VIII.

MADE UP OF VARIETIES.

1.	Mrs. Masson; or, Disorder and Apologies	135
2.	Employment for all the Faculties	141
3.	Self-Knowledge	145
4.	Crow-Bar Dignity	146
5.	A Wasted and Barren Life	147
6.	Unexpected Visitors, and What Came of it	149

	PAGE.
7. Frank's Remonstrance	154
8. Scraps about Persons and Things	156

CHAPTER IX.

EXPERIENCE OF A SICK HOUSEKEEPER.

1. Chills and Fever	160
2. About a Doctor and a Nurse	165
3. Aunt Betsey and the Irish Girl	168
4. The Progress of Hostilities	172
5. The Denouement	175

CHAPTER X.

TALKS, ACTS, AND REFLECTIONS.

1. Father Braden and Miss Leslie's Cook Book	179
2. Lending Books	183
3. Good Advice in Rhyme	185
4. Economy in Littles	186
5. Live in a Cheerful Room	189
6. Maffat the Cruel Butcher	191

CHAPTER XI.

SURPRISES AND BLESSINGS.

1. A Visit from my Parents	195
2. A Small House not an Evil in Itself	201
3. Sarah Griffith	202
4. Tarnished by the Rust of Gain	203

CONTENTS.

		PAGE.
5.	Moods in Writing or Conversation	205
6.	Importance of Trifles	208
7.	A Visit to my Childhood's Home	210
8.	Reading Books, and Observing Men	212
9.	A few Thoughts Concerning Naturalness and Affectation	214
10.	Darkened Rooms and Health	217

CHAPTER XII.

BOARDING AT MRS. PARKINSON'S.

1.	A New State of Affairs	220
2.	Scheming to Live Genteelly	223
3.	The Blessed Fortune of Having Friends	227
4.	Social and Self-Culture	229
5.	The Art of Conversation	230
6.	William Marcy; or, a Warning Incident	237
7.	James Rogers, and Obadiah Ellsworth	242

CHAPTER XIII.

THOUGHTS AND PERSONS.

1.	The Face and the Thoughts; or, the Soul Revealed in the Countenance	246
2.	Trying to Seem Young	248
3.	Injudicious Friends	250
4.	Innate Refinement	252
5.	Judge Alden; or, the Self-Made Man in Power.	256

CHAPTER XIV.

MY JOTTINGS ENDED.

PAGE.
1. DISAGREEABLE PEOPLE; AND HOW TO GET ALONG WITH THEM 266
2. BENEFIT OF WRITING 271
3. HENRY MAYBERRY'S WEDDING 273
4. POPPING CORN 274
5. THE SELFISH 276
6. KINDNESS TO ANIMALS 277
7. FAREWELL 281

JOTTINGS FROM LIFE.

CHAPTER I.

TILL I ENTERED THE ITINERANCY.

PARENTS AND EARLY LIFE.

I WAS an only daughter. My father was a deacon of the Presbyterian Church, a Justice of the Peace, and, though not wealthy, he possessed more property than most of his neighbors; therefore "Squire Strickland" was much looked up to in B., the little village where my girlhood was spent. I was a much-indulged child at home, and at school and elsewhere in the neighborhood was treated with much consideration, my opinions being regarded as of importance. This was owing probably more to the position of my father than to any peculiar merit of my own; and I mention these things because they had an effect upon the formation of my character, making it difficult for me many times in after life to endure privations, or submit to disapproval, which would have been little felt by one differently nurtured.

My life passed very quietly at home till I was about eighteen. I assisted my mother some in her household labors, but knew little of care, and had never been required to make sacrifices for others, except when it was a pleasure to me to do so. My father thought marriage the proper destiny of woman; so, when he considered me of suitable age, he selected from among the young men of our acquaintance the one he regarded most eligible for a son-in-law, and then was continually sounding his praises in my ears. Young Higley was assiduous in his attentions to me, backed by the approval of my father; but, owing to the perversity of woman's nature, or the waywardness of woman's heart in particular, or possibly, joined with these, my own peculiar repugnance to being coerced, the more highly he was extolled by my father the lower he fell in my regard. My father had been so much accustomed to having his will and opinion law, both at home and abroad, that he probably never dreamed of my permanently standing out against them; and, as my mother afterward told me, he attributed the aversion I manifested to girlish caprice, which would soon pass away, and I would eventually become the wife of Higley.

CHOICE AMONG LOVERS.

About this time there came a young man to study in the office of the village doctor. His name was Francis Edmonds, and, though a stranger in the village, being of prepossessing person and manners, he soon made one at our social gatherings. In personal appearance he presented a perfect contrast to young Higley. He was tall and dark, and had a well-developed figure, and a fine, open face, while Higley was small in stature, and had a diminutive expression of countenance. Edmonds, too, had a full, rich voice, which, as has been said of Emerson's, sounded "as if there was a man behind it," while that of Higley was weak, thin, and squeaking. I fell to comparing them in my mind the very first time I met Edmonds; not with any view to making a conquest of him, but as he surpassed in manly beauty any young man I had ever before met, while Higley, in my eyes, was the most disagreeable, I could not help contrasting them.

But Higley had one merit that outweighed all else in the mind of my father; he had wealth, and this Edmonds lacked. He was poor, an orphan, and had his own way to make in the world.

As my married life is that with which I have most to do, I will hasten over the events that preceded it. Edmonds soon expressed a regard for me, which I acknowledged was reciprocated. My father saw how matters stood, and was displeased; but this, instead of estranging, seemed to draw us nearer together. Francis had long had a leaning that way, and before the first year of his medical studies had closed he abandoned them for preparations for the Methodist ministry. Nothing could have more displeased my father. He had a prejudice against Methodists in general, and a very strong dislike to the itinerancy; and that "a wandering Methodist preacher" would become the husband of his Laura was a calamity of which he had probably never dreamed. He said many severe things, which I am disposed to forget.

My mother did not oppose my determination. I had made my own choice, she said, and must abide the consequences. But she often spoke of the trials to which the wives of itinerant ministers are subjected. This was well, that I might not be unprepared to meet them. The frightful pictures my father held up were too overdrawn to impress me as realities.

I had been a member of the Presbyterian

Church since childhood, but two years before meeting Edmonds, visiting the family of an uncle who were Methodists, I acquired a preference for the doctrines of that Church, and had often displeased my father by avowing it; therefore I did no violence to my feelings by embracing them. I told my father that, in the words of another, I thought it was better to "marry a man without money, than money without a man;" and even if the picture held up to me of the hardships I must encounter in doing so were real, it would be the fairer lot of the two.

HOME LEAVING.

We were married early one September morning, and set off for S., about fifty miles distant, the field of labor that had been assigned to Frank. How vividly every event of that day, every phase of feeling I experienced, each aspect of nature, is imprinted in my memory! We made the journey in a buggy, drawn by a beautiful chestnut pony, which a wealthy bachelor uncle had presented to my husband "to itinerate on," as he said. Some cheap furniture, bought with money which Frank had earned teaching school—for my father had refused to give us any thing—had before been sent by canal to our place of destination.

When my mother took leave of me she slipped into my hand a purse with twenty dollars of her own savings, and she had supplied me well with clothing. I shed some natural tears at leaving home and friends—my mother more than all; but the great love and hope in my heart outweighed all my regret. The day upon which we set forth was beautiful—one of the days I love best, when the bright glare of the sunlight is subdued by a slight haziness in the atmosphere. It was like my happiness, I thought, shadowed by the unpleasant circumstances attending my marriage; yet, as I sat by the side of him for whom I had given up so much, I was content, and had no fears for the future.

2

CHAPTER II.

OUR FIRST CIRCUIT.

FARMER GRIFFITH'S.

It was nearly dark when we arrived at S. By previous arrangement we were to spend the night at the house of a farmer about half a mile from the village, and, in the morning, unpack the goods that awaited us, and prepare for housekeeping in whatever tenement had been assigned us. I was very tired when we reached farmer Griffith's and drove into the spacious yard in front, the large gate of which had been swung aside to admit us by one of his sons, who was in the yard chopping, and saw us approaching. As we were driving in the door of the farm-house opened, and the farmer and two more of his sons came out to greet us. "Glad to see ye!" he exclaimed in a bluff, hearty tone.

"A'most given up yer comin' to-night. Glad ye got along," and after shaking hands with my husband, he assisted me to alight upon a log lying along side of the path.

"Walk right in; the boys 'll take care o' yer horse." Then speaking to a stout youth of some fifteen years: "Jason, bring along some more wood and put on the fire; it's a growin' chilly." We followed him into the house, he inquiring about our journey and Frank's father, for they had been companions in boyhood, and it was for this old-acquaintance' sake that we made the house of farmer Griffith our stopping-place, together with the fact that he was one of the most wealthy and influential members of the connection in that region. A bright wood fire was blazing in the spacious fireplace of the large, uncarpeted room into which we were ushered, lighting it up with a cheerful glow. As a tall girl with fair hair and a pleasant expression of countenance came forward to assist me in removing my things—"This," said the farmer, "is my oldest daughter, Sarah; and a pretty good girl she is, too." I looked into her clear, bright eyes, and thought his words needed no further confirmation. "Mother," he said apologetically, "will be in pretty soon. She's takin' care of her milk—thinks nobody can 'tend to it right but herself." "Mother" referred to his wife and the mother of the family of boys and girls growing up around him, and at this moment she came in, with a hurried manner, smoothing down the clean apron which had evidently been tied on for my reception.

"O, here she comes!" was all the introduction given by the farmer, or needed; for the good woman came up and shook my hand cordially, and she looked so kind and motherly that I felt as if I could call her "mother," too, with a right good will. She was a small, black-eyed woman, with her dark hair streaked with silver, put smoothly away under a neat cap. She had that air and expression of alertness which a woman in her station acquires who has been accustomed to attend to all the wants and requirements of a large family; and her face was not without its impress of care, though not heart-care—which wears more than all. The expression was merely anxiety for the physical wants and convenience of those dependent upon her. When she expressed solicitude for my comfort and fears that I was cold, and tired, and hungry, I felt that with her these were not mere conventional phrases.

"R'aly sorry you did n't come sooner," said Mr. Griffith. "We waited till we thought you would n't come, and then we eat supper. Lucy and her husband came home to-day to see us, and wanted to get back to their little ones afore dark. We expected you airly in the afternoon accordin' to your letter. Mother had a capital chicken-pie; but the young ones have pretty much finished it. Sharp appetites the youngsters have; but I 'd rather feed a dozen such than one puny, sickly one. But mother 'll fix up something for you. Set up closer to the fire; you look as blue as whetstones, both of you."

We begged good Mrs. Griffith not to take any trouble on our account, as we had eaten a late dinner, and did n't require it.

"Never mind me; I 'm not going to do much. You must make yourselves as comfortable as you can, while I get you a cup of tea and a mouthful of something to eat," she said pleasantly, busying herself the while stirring the fire, snuffing the candle that sat on the mantle, brushing up the ashes on the hearth, and straightening the andirons. Almost mechanically she performed these things, with the quick eye to detect and the ready hand to adjust what was out of order, which habitual supervision of all the details of a large household had given her.

"Your little wife do n't look as if she 'd seen much hardship," she said to Frank; "but she 'll get used to it before she 's been a Methodist minister's wife many years;" and after directing Sarah to set the table while she went into the kitchen to get the rest ready, she left the room. Sarah set about doing what she was bidden, and the farmer took up his wife's remark, alluding to the privations of a Methodist minister's lot, and dilated upon it.

"Yes," he said, "a Methodist minister's life an't no easy bairth, nor his wife's neither. But they do n't expect that, I s'pose when they enter on 't—at least, if they're good Christians they do n't; and if any black sheep get in expectin' to have an easy time on 't, they find their own punishment, that's all; though things are betterin' with 'em late years. They do n't see the hardships they did when I first set out in Methodism. But I do n't know as it's any better for 'em. They made hardier Christians in them days than they do now. There's been a great fallin' off in that respect sence the time o' good, old John Wesley. These fair-weather Christians han't got the backbone they had in them days."

And he went on making comparisons between the past and the present, and enumerating the trials to which those are exposed who take upon them the teaching of the Gospel, and the onerous duties both of a pastor and his wife, for a conscientious discharge of which a strict account must be rendered; and he dwelt upon the shortcomings of those engaged in this work, many of whom he feared failed of being faithful stewards of their Master, till my spirits sank and my heart grew heavy in my bosom, breaking down the good resolutions with which I had fortified myself bravely to meet and uncomplainingly to endure whatever trials might be incident to the way of life I had chosen.

As I sat there in the light of that pleasant fire, with those kind faces around me—my husband, for whom I had forsaken father and mother, and whom I had taken for my earthly guide and counselor, by my side, and, more than all, the "God o'er head" in whom I had put my trust — a chill, dreary, desolate feeling came over me, as though I was utterly forsaken of earthly and heavenly friends. Weak and ungrateful that I am, I said to myself, "These feelings are unworthy of me. If I am disposed to faint at the outset, how shall I be found wanting when the time for action comes?—and my husband, instead of having in me one to hold up his hands, and help him in his upward and onward course, as he confidently trusts and expects, will find me a clog upon his advancement—a stumbling-block in his path."

I was glad when supper came in, to give a turn to the conversation and the current of my thoughts. We made a hearty meal of the nice ham, snowy bread, and fragrant tea, flanked by a plentiful supply of pies, preserves, and doughnuts, set before us by our kind hostess; and so much is the state of the mind dependent upon the condition of these feeble bodies of ours, my spirit was less burdened when, after becoming a little rested and refreshed by this good cheer, we drew up to the fire again.

SELF-COMMUNINGS.

Mention being made of the house destined for our use—one they had been fitting up and repairing for us, as there was no parsonage at S. then—Mr. Griffith said it was not as good as it might be, still it was quite a snug, comfortable little cage for my husband to put his bird in. Ten to one we should find worse oftener than better in our journeying pilgrimage. I could not help having an unpleasant cord struck whenever the good man, in his blunt way, alluded to the hardships of a minister's life, though I tried to look as if I had expected it all, and to make myself believe so. I could scarcely have been placed in circumstances more uncomfortable or endured greater privations than my father had tried to make me believe I would meet in my chosen lot. But I fear a rose-colored mist, born of love, and hope, and youth, threw a brightness over the pictures he held up to my imagination, softening their repulsive features.

I was glad to go to bed early, and was shown by Sarah into a neat little room in a wing of the house. I knew I should like Sarah. She had a frank, honest, pleasant face, and there was an air of native refinement about her which might have been envied by many whose polish of manners has been "learned at school." She set down the candle and went out, after inquiring if there was any thing I wanted. But for the shyness she exhibited, I would have liked to have had a little chat with her, and made some inquiries about the neighborhood; but this, I thought, would wear off upon acquaintance, and we should have many pleasant times together.

As I lay there alone, the white, bare walls of the little room seemed to strike a chill to my heart. Fears and doubts took possession of my mind again; my whole future life, thickly studded with hardships, and privations, and weariness of spirit, and sundry burdens grievous to be borne, loomed up before my imagination in frightful distinctness. It had all seemed as a dream before—something far away and faintly shadowed. Now, as I lay there alone, I shuddered at the startling panorama that passed before my mental vision. I wondered how I had ever dared to brave the displeasure of my father, and the difficulties that surely awaited me in my chosen future. I offered up that night an earnest prayer for hope in good, for resignation to inevitable ill. "Save me from sinking!" was the cry that went up from my soul, and in its depths I planted a firm resolve to do what I could. And the surging tide of rebellious feeling rolled back, sweet peace stole into my soul, and then sleep with gentle fingers came and locked my senses.

THE NEXT MORNING.

When I woke the next morning my husband had already risen and left the room. I hastened to dress, fearing they might wait breakfast for me; for I knew farmers' families were in the habit of rising early — a habit not altogether consonant with my own inclination or usage at that time. There was a feeling of praise and thanksgiving in my heart on that morning. "Thank God for the sunshine!" I fervently ejaculated, as it streamed brightly in at the window of my little room. When all nature is glad shall we alone be sad?

There came a light tap at the door, and before I had time to answer it the sweet, bright face of Sarah peeped in. It was in harmony with the morning and my feelings; and, as I gave her a cordial kiss, I mentally exclaimed, "Thank God for one of his choicest blessings, true and loving hearts!"

They had breakfasted, she told me, but did not disturb me because I had been so tired the night before. They thought I would not like to get up and eat by candlelight, as was their usual custom. And indeed I should not. I remember often, when required to do so, I had repeated the words of Miss Landon, "Tell me not of the happiness of life when every morning must commence with a sacrifice." "This is one of the habits I must reform," I said to myself; "I will *make a note of it.*" My husband, Sarah said, had gone out with her father and the boys to look at the cows, with a view of selecting one for our use. "But I told mother I would bake you some cakes and make you some coffee when you got up."

I expressed a fear that I was giving her too much trouble.

"O, no," she said, frankly; "I would rather do it for you than not."

I believed her. Her clear eyes testified that it was no conventional phrase spoken from habit, but warm and direct from the heart. Mrs. Griffith, coming in from the kitchen with her sleeves rolled up and her clean check apron on, gave me a kind and motherly good-morning, and inquired how I had rested. She stood and talked with me a little while about *our prospects*, while Sarah got my breakfast ready. I shall never forget how I enjoyed that meal. It was nice and delicate in itself; the light buckwheat-cakes, and clear honey, and amber-colored coffee, and then the bright morning, the bright fire, and the brighter face of Sarah, with the serenity of spirit I had attained, all contributed to enliven me, and make me feel comfortable and happy.

"I must not suffer these fluctuations of feeling," I said to myself. "The world is no better nor brighter, no less thickly set with difficulties, than it was last night, yet how differently it looks to me!"

THE PARSONAGE.

Accompanied by farmer Griffith, his wife, Sarah, and three of "the boys"—strapping fellows, whose ages ranged from twenty-five to thirty—to help unpack and set up our furniture, we went over to the village to look at our house, and put it in readiness to live in. It was a small one, and had once been painted white. There was a pleasant yard, with a few bushes in front, and a neglected garden-spot in the rear. There were two small rooms below stairs in the main building, and a little kitchen and pantry built on behind, rather roughly, but they were snug and convenient. The walls of the front rooms were nicely plastered and whitewashed, and the floors smooth and white. The upper part of the house was unpartitioned and unfinished; its bare rafters and walls hung with cobweb drapery. But the view from the windows was pleasant, and I thought, it will do to stow away things in, and for a sleeping-room in an emergency, and was disposed to be contented with it.

The house had not been open long before we saw several persons coming up the path toward it. Mrs. Griffith, looking from the window, told us they were some of the neighboring members of our Church, who were coming to welcome us, and probably to assist if needed. And so it proved. They all set to work, and in a little time a second-hand cooking-stove that had been procured for us was blazing away in the kitchen with an at-home air; the rag-carpet was nailed down in the larger room, and a few yards that remained put down by the side of the bed set up and nicely spread in the other, which was to serve for our sleeping-room. The bed and furniture of this were those of my own little room at home—my mother having managed to smuggle them in with the rest of our goods.

We had several invitations to dinner, but, some one proposing it, decided to make a picnic dinner where we were; so Jason Griffith was dispatched home for a basket of good things. Others contributed, and we had a very pleasant and jovial meal.

A little stove Frank had used while studying was set up in the large room, which we dignified by the name of "parlor;" the dishes were arranged in the cupboard; curtains hung; and before night things began to assume quite a homelike appearance. The most trivial circumstances connected with my first setting out in the path that afterward became familiar to me, are stamped upon my memory with a distinctness which many more recent and important incidents lack. They were fixed and colored by the vividness of my feelings at that time, and assume an importance which does not intrinsically belong to them. They may not be altogether devoid of interest for some who have had similar experiences; therefore I have indulged in their detail.

THE VILLAGE.

The little village had about five hundred inhabitants, and though the streets were irregular, and it had few tasteful buildings, the site was pleasant; and I said, "'Tis home where the heart is," and felt that I could be happy there.

As I sat alone in my little room on the night after we took possession of our house, while Frank had gone out to make some necessary purchases, I said to myself, "You have entered upon a new scene of life. Instead of looking for approval every-where, you must expect to have your conduct scanned; instead of having all your wishes gratified, you must study now to please others, and may not relax your efforts even though they are often unsuccessful and unappreciated. You have heretofore lived carelessly, as whim or inclination prompted; you must now be ever ready for your duty, though sacrifice attend it; you are not your own any longer."

NEW RESOLUTIONS VERSUS OLD HABITS.

I could not help having a great many lonely hours at first when my husband was absent or engaged in study; but I had entered in earnest upon a course of reading which I thought would discipline my mind, and instruct me in the duties of my position; and I tried to make this, with my necessary employments, fill all my vacant hours, and confine my wandering thoughts, but did not always succeed at the outset. My old habits were stronger than my new resolves, and I often found myself longing to break the "Bastile bars" of my condition and leap into former freedom. These feelings, however, were transitory. My strong will-power, which had sometimes led me wrong, I brought to my aid now to subdue my waywardness of spirit. Sarah visited me occasionally, and was always welcome; but she did not spend as much time with me as I could have desired, on account of the ill-health of her mother. The farmer said he was not much of a visitor, but he dropped in sometimes when he came to the village, often bringing with him a little present of fruit, or perhaps a ham, a chicken, or a basket of eggs.

At first I felt as if there was something degrading in receiving presents of food in that way; but I tried to put away this feeling, thinking it might proceed from false pride; besides, necessity assisted my reasoning upon the point, for the horn of plenty is not *always* poured upon a minister's threshold. I got along very well with my housekeeping. Frank not only rendered me all the assistance in his power, but was very lenient to my shortcomings in housewifery; besides, he fancied himself competent to bestow upon me some lessons in this science, having "kept house" himself while studying, and made many valuable discoveries in culinary art by the aid of that necessity which assists invention. So we jogged along very amicably with respect to household management; he willing to overlook my errors in return for the deference I paid to his skill. It was something like playing at keeping house.

CHAPTER III.

SUNDRY JOTTINGS TO FILL OUT.

FRANK'S COUSIN.

FRANK had one appointment so far from home that, in bad weather, he was obliged to stay away all night. I did not like to stay alone, nor to be always dependent upon neighbors; so Henry Mayberry, a young cousin of Frank's, was invited to spend the Winter with us, and pursue his studies under Frank's supervision, which we knew he would be glad to do. A favorable and grateful response was received, and was soon followed by his arrival. Henry was eighteen — hopeful, sanguine, disposed to be "*jolly*" under the most discouraging circumstances. Many a time has he lighted up our little home with the sunshine of cheerfulness when, but for him, owing to my desponding moods, shadows would have fallen all about us. I gratefully remember many instances of this sort; and if I did not then always appreciate the sunniness of temper that threw its radiance across my pathway, the remembrance of his kind solicitude for my happiness—manifested in the most effectual way possible, by reflecting upon me the brightness of his own spirit—is recorded in my heart among its dearest memories. We received much kindness at S., not only at the hands of our own people, but from those not of our Church.

WIDOW BARKER.

I had naturally strong antipathies and partialities; but I tried to suppress any offensive manifestation of preference, lest hard feelings should arise. It was not always easy for me to do so, for I am by nature ardent in friendship, and sometimes feel—or used to—unconquerable aversion to well-meaning people not just to my taste. Among the young people especially, there were some upon whom I felt inclined to lavish much affection, while others, equally deserving and very kind to me, I should have felt disposed to keep away from me, for their presence, instead of pleasing, was wearisome and exhausting. From this cause arose some of the most serious trials I had to encounter in the beginning.

I remember a trial of this sort that occurred to me at S. My nearest neighbor was a widow Barker. She was childless, and had a competence that placed her above exertion, which left her leisure to supervise the affairs of her neighbors. When I came I was a new subject, and the widow Barker, who soon made my acquaintance, seemed to think that I ought to submit to her direction in all things. Now, it was not easy for me to submit implicitly to the direction of any one; though to those who had undoubted claims of duty or affection upon me I could concede a good deal. I owned no such allegiance to Mrs. Barker; besides, her petty meddlings in my affairs had inspired me with a strong aversion to her, which I could ill conceal, though she was very kind to her *subjects*, and if you became passive in her hands there was danger of being overwhelmed by her favors. Frank used to remonstrate with me upon my dislike to this woman, and to endeavor to convince me that to conciliate her was a matter of duty as well as interest. "Frank," I thought, "is of a more flexible disposition—easily yields his personality to others; therefore he does not know the trials these things are to me."

It is wonderful to me, on looking back now, how nervous I became about the widow Barker's supervision of my conduct. She lived directly opposite, and whenever I went out I could *feel* her black eyes watching me from her window, to see if she could detect, in my dress or deportment, any thing upon which to hang a censure. I seldom dressed without a forethought of her scrutiny; for at Church and elsewhere, I felt that she was taking note of my apparel, to see if I had had a proper regard for economy, or had failed on the score of neatness, for she was painfully, *uncomfortably* neat, and could make no allowance for the least failure on this point in others. I can not say that this surveillance was altogether without its benefits, for I fear I was inclined to be careless sometimes with regard to the proper adjustment of my dress; so it is possible I received a compensation for the annoyance it gave me in its tendency to correct my habits.

SELF-IMPROVEMENT.

We staid two years at S., and during this time I did not enter upon a systematic plan of recording my thoughts and experiences, though it was my wish and endeavor to do so. But there were so many things new in my life—so much to which I had not been accustomed to occupy my head, my heart, and my hands, that the record of this period is broken, disjointed, and incoherent. I improved some in composition by the efforts I made, and I had always had a fondness for it; and the practice of setting down my feelings and conduct when I feared they were wrong assisted me to gain the self-knowledge at which I aimed, and to correct errors of life. Still, my thoughts at this time mostly centered toward self—were much occupied by my own petty cares, and the surface of things around me. Since then I have endeavored to take a wider observation of life, and to look deeper inward.

GROWING TOLERANT.

I am more inclined to be tolerant toward offenders, as I hope for leniency to my own errors and weaknesses, and am disposed to bring home to myself the fable of the traveler who asked a night's shelter from some one who was unwilling to harbor the wayfarer because of his unworthiness. An angel appeared, and rebuked the inhospitable man in this wise: "Has your Heavenly Father borne with this sinner for so many years, and can not you endure him for a single night?" And then my larger experience of life has taught me not to be surprised or disappointed at finding defects in character. I used to turn from one to another, vainly looking for perfection, and sometimes imagining for a time that I had found it, till some obliquity appeared, when resentful feelings would arise as if a wrong had been done me—as though I had been purposely deceived by false pretenses of excellence, when I had only been *self*-deceived; and perhaps the possessor of the fault I contemned was altogether unconscious of it, and possibly, at the same time, saw a similar one in me of which I, too, was wholly unaware.

PLEASANT MEMORIES.

Many pleasant remembrances are connected with our sojourn at S.—some sad ones, too; for it was there our little Ella was born, and there we made her grave. I have since been among those possessing greater cultivation of mind and manners; but kinder, more single-hearted people than those we fell in with at S., I never expect to meet again. They did not forget to "guard the stranger's heart," and soothe it by kind offices; and I know there are many who would extend these oftener did they realize of how much value they are to those thrown among strangers—perhaps for the first time. Their courtesy was heart-taught; and none other is genuine, though *society* may prescribe modes of manifestation. The remembrance of their sympathy and kindness warms my heart at this moment, and will remain with me to the latest hour of my life. Their primitive manners did not obscure their true goodness, nor render it any less grateful to me; and I have often since, when wearied with hollow seeming—which we must acknowledge is abroad in the world—longed to refresh my spirit with the honest simplicity of these good people.

Yet even at S. I did not wholly escape criticism of an unfavorable kind, which, no doubt, was deserved, and which exerted a favorable influence upon my conduct by making me more watchful. Even, as I have hinted, the petty persecutions of my neighbor, Mrs. Barker, which I regarded as a serious annoyance at the time, were made beneficial in correcting some of my habits, though I suspect the improvement was wrought as much from a spirit of pride as through a feeling of humility awakened by the errors presented to my view. I think I did not like to gratify the widow Barker by a sight of those flaws in my conduct for which she was evidently watching. So fault-finders sometimes work us a good they do not intend.

SARAH GRIFFITH.

Many pleasant evenings I passed at S. with cousin Harry and Sarah Griffith, reading loud to each other, or discussing some interesting topic. By this means a desire for intellectual improvement was awakened in Sarah, for which she had not before had opportunity, and the time so spent was improving to us all.

I will mention here that an attachment sprang up between Henry Mayberry and my friend Sarah Griffith, as I mentally predicted from their first acquaintance. It resulted in an engagement, and eventually in marriage—though many years intervened before this consummation, owing to some pecuniary causes which hindered his advancement to his profession, the ministry—the illness of Sarah's mother, which proved fatal, and, from her care and anxiety during this period, the decline of her own health, accompanied by a lameness, resulting, doubtless, in part, from these causes, which brought her many years of suffering. She had, besides, the peculiar trial of a step-mother—a woman of hard nature, from whom she met little sympathy; but she came forth from the ordeal of her trials so chastened and etherealized that she seemed an angel already. Strength of character she gained by her afflictions—purity she possessed before. I little thought when I first saw her, that so many changes—so much of romance, even, would come into her quiet life, partly resulting, no doubt, from her acquaintance with me.

METHODISM ONE EVERY-WHERE.

It has been said, "If you know the habits of swallows and swifts in one place, you are acquainted with the habits of swallows and swifts every-where." It is something so with things pertaining to Methodism. I heard a lady once say — not a Methodist either — that if she was away from home—felt a little home-sick, and wanted to see something that looked familiar, she always went to a Methodist meeting, if she could; because one Methodist meeting was always so like another every-where, it gave her a home-feeling to attend one. This is probably not the case now in so marked a degree as at an earlier day. Dress, the mode of worship, and other externals have been brought more to a popular standard. But the lives of itinerating ministers and that of their families are much alike in their general features. Donation parties, album quilt gatherings, and the like, are much the same every-where, and descriptions of them have often been given; so I have selected from the record of past years some of the experiences that were peculiar to myself, and some of my struggles for self-improvement.

CHAPTER IV.

OUR SECOND CIRCUIT.

A BIRD'S-EYE VIEW.

At E., where we removed next, I was not as happy as I had been at S.—dear, good, plain, old S., with its steepleless, uncarpeted church, unpretending dwellings, and sincere, warm-hearted people. A desire for show and display ruled here, to the detriment of more solid attainments, and, I fear, of those heart graces which should characterize the Christian. Not that I am averse to suitable ornaments, or the refinements of life—I am by nature, perhaps, somewhat too fond of them; but, though I am pleased with extrinsic graces, I love genuine heart-warmth better.

It is curious to note the likeness that runs through neighborhoods—how people assimilate in tastes and character by living near each other, as certain plants do by proximity. The similarity may be partly accounted for, no doubt, on the principle that "like seeks like" in making up a community. "Birds of a feather flock together," as the homely proverb goes; but I have found little communities alike in their main characteristics. Yet notwithstanding this striving for the outward that prevailed at E., I found there many friends, good and true, the remembrance of whose kindness I shall bear ever with me.

It was during our stay at E. that I began the regular practice of keeping a journal—setting down daily something from my thoughts, trials, or observations. This I thought would help me to improve, not only in language and composition, but in character and conduct. By looking back upon my thoughts and actions daguerreotyped in this way, I could judge their merits better, and by comparing them with my present feelings and conduct, use them to measure my improvement. I have never neglected a duty for the use of my pen, though it has grown to be a great pleasure to me—taken up at first from the idea that benefit would result from it, and continued many times when it was an irksome duty to me. But it has thrown a clearer light upon my outward duties, and lightened their burden, not only by its influence upon my intellect, but upon my heart. Cultivating habits of thought and reflection has assisted me to place the nearest duties first, and instructed me in the use of ways and means of performing them well; and I regard that mental culture of little worth which does not improve us in the common things of daily life. Trifles make up the sum of our existence; and it is only at rare intervals that we have the power or find the occasion of doing any great thing.

Here is something taken from some of the peculiar trials of that period—trials which have since been transmuted to pleasures, as affording an exercise for heart graces. I would not have my way all smooth. These little thorns in our way may be used as spurs to improvement.

> "Not a thorn besets our way
> That mercy could have spared."

"One of the hardest requisitions in my lot is, for me, to have it expected that I will make myself agreeable under all circumstances, and to all sorts of people, whether their society is pleasant or distasteful to me, whether it is convenient for me to receive them or otherwise, under the penalty of having it said, 'The minister's wife has queer ways, and you never know where to find her. Sometimes she seems overjoyed to see you; again, appears cold, and you do not feel welcome.' I am afraid comers-in do not always make sufficient allowance in this matter, especially for us who must be subjected to weariness of feeling; just as though any one could always be glad alike to see even the dearest friends. Can they? Are they always so? I can answer only for myself, and I must confess to varying phases of feeling. I believe it is something common to our poor humanity. Then what self-command is required to meet these exigencies that are constantly occurring! How much strength, and wisdom, and goodness we need to guide us continually in the minutest actions of our lives!

"In my present position I am more subjected to these little annoyances and interruptions, and must fortify accordingly. I must acquire more self-control in this matter; for I feel that my usefulness is sometimes sadly marred by the lack of it. I often look with wonder and no small share of admiration upon poor Frank, to see how his affability, like the widow's cruse, never grows less for the using, and I feel almost inclined to envy him. Then I try to comfort myself with the assurance that this *dead level* of feeling can not, from the very constitution of our natures, be attained by us all, and that it is all very well for Frank, because he does not have to make any sacrifice in the matter, while I should be continually crucifying some dear little preference, or be obliged to give up some darling inclination, that I might not conflict with others; and I question, 'Is it required of me?' and resolve not to decide hastily."

LITERARY GLEANINGS.

I made a rule that I would not only put down one original thought every day—something suggested by observation, reflection, or a peculiar state of feeling—but one sentence from something I had read—a few lines of poetry or a prose quotation containing some useful thought. I averaged this and something more in the course of a year; for I made it a rule to

> "Seize upon truth where'er 't is found,
> Among my friends, among my foes,
> On Christian or on heathen ground—
> The plant's divine where'er it grows."

I have been strengthened and cheered by these gleanings; they have, besides, shed light for me upon the path of duty, and smoothed it.

I usually selected something that would guide me in my search for excellence, and strengthen my resolves to attain it; for I felt that I needed all the aids in this respect that I could obtain. This practice of transcribing passages containing some moral lesson, some truth that might be of use to me in my daily life, besides grounding in my mind many valuable truths, has stimulated thought and reflection, and I have acquired by it a freer use of language. The mere beauties I met, the flowers of literature, I enjoyed in passing, but did not take time to transplant many of them. I read some books because they were standard works, because every body read them, where I found poor gleaning of the kind I desired—something that would be of use to me in my daily life.

When Henry was reading Byron and Homer—for he always took an hour or two every day for reading, outside of his regular studies, to refresh his mind, as he said—I asked him to read aloud to me when I was sewing of evenings; but among the glittering things in them I found very little that I could detach and apply to my own needs. I find only this passage set down from Homer:

> "Who dares think one thing and another tell,
> My soul detests him as the gates of hell;"

which I regarded as rather a strong protest against falsehood.

Complaining to Henry one evening, when he had been reading something pretty to me, that I could find no nutriment in it: "Well," he said, "what would you have? Nutriment always? You might as well complain of a rose because you could not boil it for dinner like a cabbage."

IN HEAVINESS OF SPIRIT.

I feel a spirit of heaviness this morning, which I have tried in vain to shake off. Can I do so? I have called reason and philosophy to my aid, but

> "The clouds will not let the sun shine through,
> Nor yet descend in rain and end."

I do not like the recurrence of these moods; they are unprofitable and unpleasant both for myself and others.

> "Be always as cheerful as ever you can,
> For no one delights in a sorrowful man."

No; nor woman either. "Though some good Samaritan may be willing to pour oil on her wounded spirit, the priest and Levite will instinctively pass by on the other side." Benevolence should prompt us to be always cheerful, that we may not throw a shadow upon the happiness of others; and the effort to appear cheerful from such motives can not fail to bring a portion of serenity to our own spirits. I do not know the spring of this dissatisfied feeling this morning, and some one has said, "If you are melancholy and do not know the cause, be assured it is some physical cause;" another, that "some duty has been left unperformed."

Perhaps an analysis of my mind may dispel

it. It is not the weather; it is bright as paradise out of doors.

"Some days will be dark and dreary,"

as Longfellow sings, though Nature smile never so sweetly. "We make the weather in our hearts," says a French writer, "whether the sun shines out or the hours are black with storms."

In spite of all my efforts at self-discipline there are days when the performance of customary duties is irksome, and I go heavily about them. I feel spiritless, languid, depressed, nervous, sometimes irritable. It is not a spiteful feeling, but as if every nerve in my body was a fine harp-string, upon which every thing around me was hammering discords — discords in themselves. Yet I think this disturbed state calls for a metaphysician much more than a physician to explain it, and point out the means for a proper adjustment. Yet how few there are skilled to "minister to a mind diseased!"

I was interrupted by a call from Mrs. Wyman. She brought sunshine with her, and left a little behind. I believe she does so wherever she goes, without in the least diminishing her own stock. She must have a fount of sunshine in her heart, supplied from some unfailing source, while the spring of *my* cheerfulness, I fear, is intermittent, subject to times and seasons — capricious, like an April sky. Heaven grant me an even flow of spirits — not rushing like the mountain torrent, then dry as desert sand. "Be really as cheerful as possible, for a sullen state is but an ungaining state, and does no good."

USES OF CENSORIOUS PERSONS.

Mrs. Matson and Mrs. Beadle called to-day. Mrs. Matson is genial, pleasant, and, I am sure, genuinely kind. I always feel on good terms with her and myself when I am with her; I feel that she appreciates and approves me. With Mrs. Beadle it is different. I have a sort of uneasy sensation, as though she were scanning one with an unfavorable eye. On the present occasion she spoke of the pastor's wife that preceded me in terms of censure. She said she visited altogether too much, to the neglect of her household matters. And then she was so wasteful that they lived very miserably, though by proper management they might have been very comfortable upon what they received. Some ministers' wives, she said, devoted themselves *too exclusively* to home, seeming to take little interest in the people and affairs of their husbands' charges. This, too, she thought, was a serious fault. A woman might help her husband greatly if she was so disposed and qualified to assist him, as she ought to be if she assumed the position of a pastor's wife.

All this is very true, I thought, but somehow the manner of her saying it grated unpleasantly upon me. Does she mean any reproof to me? I thought. In which way have I erred, and thus failed to gain the just medium she thinks proper? It is surely not in going too much; perhaps she thinks I do not take enough interest in the matters of the Church and society.

After they had gone, I thought censorious persons are of some use after all, if we will but profit by their censoriousness—reversing their process, gaining nutriment from what is poisonous, while they gather poison from the loveliest flowers. I suspect, however, that I am in danger of running to the extreme of becoming too selfish—too much absorbed by my own household cares, my own individual concerns. I must see to this, and try if I can not, without loving these less, without running any risk of neglecting those *near* duties which should have the first place in my heart, regard outside interests more. Truly this censorious spirit, though it seems

"Ugly and venomous,"

may yet bear for us

"A precious jewel in its head,"

lighting up our faults that we may see and correct them.

How truly I need—how truly we all need—some impartial and nice-judging person to tell me just how well I perform my duties, and where I fall short — to tell me exactly how I fill my position, and what my general reputation is among the people! In this case it would be a benefit to be able to

"See ourselves as others see us;"

for, though they might not always see us just as we are, we could not help gaining some profitable hints upon conduct and deportment.

It is from a desire to amend what is amiss in me, and to do the best I can, that I would learn these things. I see that other ministers' wives have reputations of different qualities, but I do not think that, in general, they are clearly aware what it is, or they would try to modify it more favorably in many instances. To tell one these things would be a truly-friendly office. Yet what friends have I who would perform it for me fully? Would they not rather gloss over my defects, and color the favorable side of my character beyond the reality? Then if we can learn our errors from the harsh and censorious, we should not despise to do so, if we desire to excel.

TIMELY GIFT.

How well I realize to-day that it is not the cost of a gift, but its timeliness that makes its value many times! Looking from the window about the middle of the afternoon, I saw a buggy drive up and stop at the gate. "Who is it?" I thought; but I saw in a moment it was old Mr. Ware and his wife from M. My first thought was, what cheer have I to set before them? I had not a mouthful of meat in the house, and I knew the old gentleman does not know how to make a meal without it. It was not the day upon which we could get it from the butcher's; besides, Frank was gone from home, and would be away till after dark. I might get some at a neighbor's, perhaps; but Frank detests borrowing—as do I, for that matter, but sometimes necessity overcomes my scruples. While I was perplexing myself with this matter, after installing them in the parlor—for I found they had had no dinner—whom should I see but Mrs. Miller's hired boy coming up the path toward the house with a basket on his arm! "My good fairy has sent me something," I thought, "to help me out of my dilemma." And sure enough, when he came in and uncovered the basket, there were a couple of nice, fat chickens, all ready to cook. On removing them, there, at the bottom of the basket, lay a dozen fresh eggs.

Nothing could have been more timely, for eggs were as great a scarcity with us as meat. Mrs. Miller had divined my very want, seeing company drive up, and knowing something of the condition of our larder as well as the state of the market. "Mrs. Miller is intuitive," I said to myself; "if I had told her my perplexity, she could not have answered it more readily or satisfactorily. I felt a spirit of lightness in a moment. "Now," I thought, "I shall not be under a cloud during the whole time of their visit." How these little things lighten one's burdens!—these little things done in the spirit of "Do to others as ye would that they should do unto you." It is this spirit, not less than the material aid received, that makes them pleasant—this is their true aroma, the odor of kindness that invests them. They "take from the heap of misery and add to the heap of happiness."

How often have I received a kindness in this way, the value of which was enhanced tenfold by the time and manner in which it was given! How often, in our passage through life, we can increase the happiness of others by these little things!—how we can smooth the little perplexities that like thorns beset their path! How much oftener would people minister to others in this way could they see and realize how much good they might do with very little sacrifice on their own part, perhaps with none at all! Once false pride would have alloyed a gift of this kind; now I consider that those who thus minister to my comfort and need will be rewarded.

CHAPTER V.

JOTTINGS IN CONTINUANCE.

WIDOW BARKER IN A NEW CHARACTER.

I MUST record a very unexpected visit I had a few weeks ago, not having any thing else very particular to write to-night. I was sitting by the fire after tea, in rather a listless mood, wishing I had a Biddy to wash up the tea-things and put matters to rights for *the night—I do have such moods occasionally. I sat there with one foot on the fender, nursing my indolence, when there came a rap at the door. I had just been thinking that I must pass a lonely evening, and did not feel much like reading, nor work either, and was rather glad of the prospect of having the monotony relieved. I went to the door, and who should be standing there but the widow Barker—that was! I could hardly believe my eyes; but there was no mistaking her black, piercing ones—though I observed at the first glance that, though unusually bright and sparkling, their *sharp* expression was softened down a little, and her face, that had looked sallow and pinched, was rosy and radiant. I greeted her rather warmly, for I felt no grudge against her for the uneasiness she had once caused me, and of which I knew she was altogether unconscious. A little man accompanied her—a very insignificant and harmless-looking little man, with small, blue eyes set far back in his head, and some straggling, light locks about his "little, wee face," and he had a "little, yellow beard," that bore a striking resemblance to a fragment of the smoke-tree in the yard. The lady turned to him with pride in her look and a patronizing air, and introduced him as "Mr. Wanyer—*my husband*," pronouncing the last two words with peculiar unction.

I must confess that this announcement rather took me by surprise, and that there was something in the tableau before me that suggested ideas of the ludicrous, though I tried to simulate a well-bred impenetrableness, and to act as if it was the most natural thing in the world for the widow Barker to have a husband—and such a husband—lest the incongruity that struck me might betray itself by my looks, which are apt to be rather tell-tale. You are not to suppose that I suffered the widow Ba—Mrs. Wanyer to stand on the steps as long as it has taken me to describe her appearance and that of her *satellite*. I convoyed her into the parlor, where I had had a little fire in the forenoon; and after establishing them comfortably, and making a few inquiries, and giving the expected gratulations, I went out to prepare a cup of tea—for I knew the lady's partiality for this beverage, hot and strong—and to make ready the table otherwise for their supper. I heard them chatting incessantly while I was about these things, and occasionally a little laugh from the bride, which evinced the supreme content of her heart.

When they came out to tea—she towing the little man after her—she still continued her patronizing air toward him, and when they sat down to the table she selected for him the choice tidbits which she said he preferred, watching as he ate them with evident enjoyment at his relish, and applauding, when he spoke, with an air that expressed *"that's a good boy!"* It was really amusing to see this couple together; and partly for the secret amusement this afforded me, and partly because I heard directly from all my good friends at S., I passed a very pleasant evening. The little man seemed to regard his strong-minded consort with very great reverence, and his little eyes would twinkle approvingly when she delivered some opinion in her oracular way, while her manner toward him was encouraging, bland, and patronizing. They spent the night with me, and in the morning went on their way rejoicing. *This was their bridal tour.*

I learned afterward that Mr. Wanyer had

come to S. on some agency—a little old bachelor who had never got on very well in worldly matters, but was very honest and well-meaning withal. The widow courted, married, and appended him to her establishment. Weak men, it is said, generally marry clever women. Not having the capacity to entertain, and perhaps guide themselves, they like somebody who can do it for them; and the widow Barker—that was—is an incessant talker, and what such men as the one she has caught up regard as a "*smart woman.*" Is n't it wonderful that these weak men usually marry a woman who will keep them in leading-strings? But it is wisely ordered, I suppose—this affinity of opposites; for how could the blind lead the blind, or the weak support the weak?

FATHER BRADEN.

Another blessing in my path, in the shape of a valuable acquaintance, or one who I feel will be so. This is an old gentleman who has been a Methodist preacher in his day, but has not preached for some years on account of ill-health. He has a competence of his own, and lives where he pleases. He is a character, an original one, and such I like. He does not pin his faith or his opinions upon other people's sleeves. Father Braden has stuff in him for a reformer, but has never figured much in that line on a large scale. He delivers himself of his opinions whenever occasion calls, and, having dropped them, leaves them to work out their own ends. He seems to have a fatherly oversight of my conduct, which is in no way offensive, for I feel that it springs from a real interest in my wellbeing and well-doing. Mrs. Miller had spoken of him to me before as a valuable acquaintance of her own, and I was particularly desirous to see him. He is at present living with a half-sister, Mrs. Alibone, who resides in the village. Flanked by two such friends as he and Mrs. Miller, in whom I may safely trust, I feel a sense of security, a confidence, that takes away from the fearfulness that sometimes besets me with regard to the way before me, and their friendship, besides, imparts to my life a pleasant glow of happiness.

Misfortunes, it is said, never come singly, but in battalions. I wonder if pleasant things do n't come so too; so many have happened to me to-day; all small, but making quite a sum of happiness in the aggregate. In the first place, a handsomely-bound volume of Mrs. Hemans's poems, from Mr. Wise. The present was grateful to me, and the friendly feeling that prompted it still more so. Then I had a cheerful, affectionate letter from home that made my heart glad. Through the kindness of considerate friends we are going to have some conveniences added to the house, and, better than all, father Braden is coming to board with us. I hope to derive both pleasure and benefit from this arrangement, for he does not hesitate to tell me when I go wrong, knowing I desire that he should do so, and then his conversation is very enlivening, as well as instructive. I wish to be good and do good as far as I can, and I must seek every method of improvement to these ends. I have many facilities for this which it would be culpable to neglect. I must attain a more equable temper, because at present I am too much at the mercy of circumstances, and these variations of mood hinder my growth in excellence.

LETTER FROM SARAH GRIFFITH.

I am just gladdened by a letter from my dear, dear friend, Sarah Griffith. Pardon me, reader, if I insert a portion of it among these jottings. True friendship is a plant of rare growth; when found do not let us cast it away. She says:

"How glad I was to get your letter! It came to me when I was in a desponding mood, and it was, O, how welcome! It seemed to speak to me in your dear voice, and I fancied I could feel your loving eyes looking tenderly and sympathizingly into mine. Many thanks, dear friend, for the consolation it gave me, for every word dropped balm.

"O, I have so longed to see you, but this lameness prevents my coming to you, and I know you can not come to me at present; so I say to my heart, 'Peace, be still,' though it does not always obey my bidding. I have found myself, I do n't know how many times to-day, repeating the lines of Young, which you and I, dear Laura, and one other loved one, learned together in those happy days when the future was so bright to me—the present all rose-colored. Do you remember them? I know you do—the days and the lines.

> "'O, for the bright complexion, cordial warmth,
> And elevating spirit of a friend!
> For twenty Summers ripening by my side—
> All peculance of falsehood long thrown down—
> All social virtues rising in his soul
> As crystal clear, and smiling as they rise.
> Here nectar flows; it sparkles in our sight—
> Rich to the taste, and genuine from the heart;
> High-flavored bliss for gods, on earth how rare—
> On earth how lost!'

"I have read much about friendship, I have thought and talked about it, but never did I so fully feel and realize the blessedness and sacredness of friendship as now. I know that you are a true friend, dear Laura. My heart rests on you with perfect confidence. I know that you feel pain at my sorrow, and would make sacrifices of your own pleasure to give me joy. This is true friendship. How blessed it is! How the conviction that it is mine strengthens me, though I may not hear these sweet assurances breathed from your lips, nor receive the tender ministrations that I know you would gladly bestow. 'There is a great deal of vital air in loving words,' and to *feel* that we are loved brings peace and comfort too."

CONQUERING SELF.

I am, it seems to me, the only discordant element in our little household. Father Braden is always calm and serene; Henry ever cheerful and lively, overflowing with good-humor, even when he has much cause for sadness, and Frank invariably placid, equable, harmonious, while my spirits rise and fall like the tides—I fear without sufficient cause. I try to excuse myself to myself, and say it is because I

> "Have not the art
> To smile when discontent sits heavy at my heart."

And then my better sense steps in, and asks, "Wherefore the need of her sitting there at all—this unwelcome and unprofitable guest, that makes your burdens heavier, and casts a mildew upon all your joys? Why suffer these depressions, that are due more to an inward influence than to an outside irresistible power? Have you not strength within you for the mastery?"

And then, listening to this bold questioner, I say humbly, "I must see to this. If the strength rests within me to modify and control these varying moods, I must exert it, for they often conflict seriously with my interest, my pleasure, and the performance of duty. 'Know thyself—

govern thyself' shall be my motto; for unless I *do* learn self-discipline—obtain control of this little principality of passions, and desires, and selfish feelings in my own breast, how can I ever hope to be successful in influencing others?—and I a missionary! I have always been averse to surrendering to any outside power; shall I be overcome by insidious foes from within? Rule shall be given to those powers of my nature to which rule is due. These 'unpassed Alps' of pride, and passion, and stubborness must not bar my progress to excellence."

CHITCHAT ABOUT FEMALE AUTHORS.

We were talking to-day—father Braden, Mrs. Miller, Frank, and I—about female writers; and in the course of the conversation something transpired about my writing. Mrs. Miller was pleased to compliment me upon it—I have sometimes allowed her to see some portions of what I had written; and she playfully asked Frank if he knew how nearly allied he was to "that dim horror, a literary woman," and further, that there was danger he might be put in a book some day. Frank replied, in the same vein, that he would beg to be spared this particular mode of immortality, especially if one had got to have his name embalmed by his wife while he was still living.

"Ah, jealousy!" laughed Mrs. Miller. "Men do not like to be outshone by their wives."

"Never fear," I said; "should I write a book I will be very careful about exhibiting you to view. I would not like to undertake so difficult a subject; so you need not fear being immortalized by my pen."

He would much prefer, he said, achieving his own immortality in this particular direction; and then we talked a good deal about literary women, and men, too, and their peculiarities.

A TALK ABOUT THE ITINERANCY.

Mr. Miller came in this evening; and we had a little conversation about the itinerancy—the advantages and disadvantages attending it. Father Braden said, what I fear is too true, that though the system is favorable to the highest improvement, ministers—many of them—were very lax about availing themselves of its peculiar privileges, and in consequence often failed to improve themselves or benefit their hearers as they ought.

Mr. Miller asked if the *certainty* of a place did not with some foster ease and indolence; and if the fear of losing it through unfitness would not with many be a salutary stimulant to proper exertions in self-culture, that they might acquit themselves with credit in the pulpit, and render their preaching more effective. They had considerable argument, *pro* and *con*.

Father Braden admitted that many were guilty of defects in pronunciation and grammatical inaccuracies, which were altogether inexcusable, because a man can attain correct language outside of schools; and bungling in this particular would mar the beauty and hinder the efficiency of a sermon which might otherwise possess much merit.

Mr. Miller said he had heard sermons, in other respects very good, defective in proper language to a degree that excited emotions of the ludicrous instead of rousing devotional ones; and the whole effect was spoiled by blemishes of this sort that might easily have been avoided. And then they indulged in some pleasantries at the expense of the itinerant system, though father Braden and Mrs. Miller firmly believe in it.

Mrs. Miller remarked that the sense of security a Methodist minister felt with regard to a provision for the future was worth a great deal in some respects that were not down in the books. She thought it contributed to serenity of mind and development of person. Methodist ministers—the most of them—were comfortable-looking—on pretty good terms with themselves and the world in general. They were free from the haggard, care-worn look of most business men or ministers of other denominations—they looked as though they had good digestion.

I repeated a proverb, that "Content is the mother of good digestion;" and she said she had no doubt that freedom from care and anxiety about the future contributed to produce the results she had spoken of. She mentioned the case of a friend of hers—a lean, sallow-looking man, who had been a dry-goods' clerk. He became a Methodist minister. Passing through the village where he lived, a few years afterward, she called to see him, and could scarcely recognize, in the portly, contented-looking personage who presented himself, any resemblance to her former cadaverous, anxious-looking friend.

Father Braden said that the sense of "security" spoken of reminded him of what a man once said about his salary: "There is one advantage I have found in living on a salary," said he; "it relieves one's mind from great anxiety—*it is a certain thing.* Before my income was fixed I was perpetually fearing that I should not be able, at the end of the year, to meet my expenses. Now I *know* I shall not!"

Mrs. Miller remarked that she supposed it was this *sense of security* with regard to a provision for their necessities, that promoted tranquillity of mind in paupers, and therefore made them long-lived, as statistics showed they were—though she said she did not intend any comparison by this.

SABBATH EVENING THOUGHTS.

It is Sabbath evening—one of those beautiful evenings which all have seen and some have felt. The moon, like a pure spirit looking down from its heavenly dwelling-place, sheds a benign influence on all around, and her light seems to pervade the soul. At such an hour as this

"The divinity stirs within us;"

and we feel that—

"Dust thou art, to dust returnest,
Was not spoken of the soul."

While I was sitting by the open window, enjoying the beauty of the night, writing those words, Mrs. Miller came in. She said, "This is indeed a 'beautiful world of ours;' and were the moral world in unison with the physical, we should have, what we all have so ardently desired and devoutly prayed for,

'A heaven on earth begun.'"

And then we spoke of the millennium—that glorious period when one universal Sabbath shall prevail on earth. It is a subject which has often occupied my reflections, and one upon which the mind delights to dwell. I have often pictured to myself this period, during which the earthquake and the tempest would no more rage, when sin and sorrow should cease, and all men become a band of brothers. Not only shall the viler passions be banished, but doubt and prejudice, and suspicion and deceit, that now "spread themselves 'twixt man and man, an everlasting mist."

When I was alone again my thoughts assumed a form somewhat like the following:

> O, for that glorious jubilee's bright birth,
> When sin's foul image shall be banished earth!
> O, for the dawning of that glorious day,
> When every evil shall be swept away!
> Then shall the galling bonds of sin be riven—
> Then shall a flood of glorious light from heaven
> Illume our darkened souls. Bright jubilee!
> O, when shall we thy glorious dawning see?
> No tempests then shall frown—no clouds arise
> To dim the brightness of our Summer skies;
> Man shall not war with man, nor plagues destroy—
> All will be love, and harmony, and joy.
> Then shall Hypocrisy's dark mantle fall;
> Peace spread her downy wings and reign o'er all;
> The glorious Sun of Righteousness shall rise,
> Dispel these fogs of sin which dim our skies;
> His healing beams to earth's remotest bound
> Shall spread, diffusing light on all around.

THE MINISTER'S WIFE AT A PARTY.

We were invited last night to a little social gathering at the widow Matson's. It is the first time I have been out in any general society since I came here. It was perhaps weak in me, but I must confess I felt very nervous about going; nervous—I do n't know any better term to express an indefinite, uneasy sensation—all the time I was there.

There were about twenty persons present. Most of them I had met before, but many of them only in a formal way, when we exchanged calls, at Church, etc. Now, I felt, was going to be the trial time with me, and I was so afraid I should n't appear to good advantage, should make an unfavorable impression, cause invidious criticism in some way, that I am sure the fear must have been parent of the result. "First impressions are lasting," I thought. "Every body will be watching the minister's wife, and speaking to others of what she says and does. If I once establish a character for agreeability and propriety of deportment, the way will be easy afterward. I have seen that, after certain qualities are attributed to a person by universal consent, it takes very little effort to keep up a reputation for them. I am going to record all my weakness; perhaps it will help me to conquer it in the future, if I keep it staring me in the face."

My judgment tells me it is well to avoid improprieties of behavior, for reputation's sake, and for the influence of our example upon others; but my good sense also tells me that we should not suffer a restless anxiety upon this point to defeat the very end at which we aim; but I am sure my feverish uneasiness last night must have produced this result. We should desire to please; this is the groundwork of an agreeable manner, but too visible an effort spoils the effect. How well I know this! Yet we have not always strength to act up to our convictions of what is right and proper, and best for us. To keep before one the idea, "*I am the center of observation,*" unfavorable or otherwise, will detract from both ease and dignity.

I had an hour of worry and uncertainty before I went. *What to wear,* was the important question to decide—fearful I should dress too much or too little. I brought out my black silk and my brown silk, and tried to settle the matter by looking at them, and imagining how I should look in each. The brown silk is trimmed with rich lace that aunt Hattie gave me, and is just as it was made a few months before I was married, but it is as good as new. I was afraid the lace would look too extravagant and showy—I couldn't explain, "*My aunt gave it to me*"—so I concluded to put on my black silk. "A black silk," I said to myself, "is suitable for almost any occasion; so I shall be safe wearing it."

Putting the glass down on the floor, just before I was ready to go, to see if all was right *round the bottom*, I saw, or thought I did, that my dress was too short. Nothing makes one look more dowdyish than a short dress when long ones are worn, I decided, and the personal appearance *is* of some importance; so I hurried it off and put on my merino, for I heard Frank coming down stairs then, expecting of course to find me all ready, as I had appeared to be an hour before. I presented myself to him in a moment, dress on, collar pinned, and shawl and bonnet in hand.

"Why, I thought you were dressed in black a little while ago," he said; "all rigged from top to toe."

"Well, so I was." I hesitated—men do n't understand these things, I thought. "But my black silk was so short," I went on, "I did n't like to wear it the first time I went out. It was long enough when it was made, but fashions change. One feels so awkward in a short dress when long ones are worn; and I want to appear as well as I can to-night, you know." And I tried to laugh, but felt a little ashamed withal.

"Too short!" he exclaimed. "I thought it was just a respectable length. I'm not much of a judge of ladies' dress, but it seems to me a plain black dress always looks better than any thing else, especially for you. But it does n't matter; the dress you have on looks well enough. We must be off or we shall be late, I fear."

If I had n't been ashamed to I should have said, "Stop a moment and let me change it now." I felt a strong inclination to do so, but I suppressed the expression of it, and followed Frank out to the buggy, thinking again, men do n't understand these things—it is n't worth while talking. "Perhaps it is n't too short after all," I thought; "I only imagined so. I *do* always feel best in a black dress, and I am sure *look* best, and nothing certainly can be more suitable." And then I felt uneasy all the way because I had not worn another dress, though I did n't say any thing more about it. I shrank from having all my weakness known.

The company presented quite a gay and fashionable appearance—much more so than I had expected to see. After the introductions were gone through with, and I looked around and saw that most of the ladies were dressed in silk of one kind or another, I suffered the fact that I, a stranger, had on a merino, far from new, to detract from the enjoyment I should otherwise have derived from the party, which was very pleasant. It added, too, to the little flurry of spirits I felt at appearing among strangers for the first time, and to the self-consciousness, of which, when I am a little nervous, I have too large a share. It increased the doubt with regard to "How do I appear?" "What will they think of me?" and took away from the serenity and self-possession of my manner.

Now I have made a resolution that I will not suffer the equal poise of my mind to be disturbed by these trifling annoyances that must sometimes occur to us all, guard against them as we will. I did not tell Frank all the disagreeable feelings I had had from so slight a cause; I was ashamed to; but I said to him after we got home, "It seems to me I appeared very ill to-night. Did n't I?"

"Why, I didn't see any thing unusual in your appearance," he answered, unsatisfactorily, which I thought, at least, rather an equivocal compliment.

CHAPTER VI.

AT ANOTHER POST.

MAKING AND PARTING FROM FRIENDS.

SETTLED again in another post, the pleasant village of F. Every thing seems favorable so far as externals are concerned. There is an air of business and bustle about the place that is enlivening after living in prosy E. I like life; it keeps one's faculties astir. I have felt very contented since we came here, thus far. Human nature I expect to find here in its usual variety of phases. I shall doubtless make friends as I have done in other places, and leave them again, though I would fain "grapple them to my soul with hooks of steel." I shall incur censure too, as who can avoid it, let him do the best; but this will also become dim with time and absence; so, should I return in a few years, I might find friendships and enmities reduced to a similar level.

We are very pleasantly situated here in our household arrangements, having "kitchen, parlor, and hall" separate, which is not always found by our migratory class, nor can we expect it. There is one advantage, though, in living in a poor house—it makes us enjoy a good one when we get it. As some one said to a person who complained of a bad house he had rented of him, "You will take pleasure in it when you are out of it." So there is a compensation in every thing. The ill we suffer makes us enjoy with greater zest the good that falls in our way.

HENRY AGAIN WITH US.

Henry is with us again. He has taken a school about two miles from the village, and will spend his Sabbaths with us. He is sobered somewhat since he came to us first; though no untoward circumstances, I think, could entirely obliterate the fine vein of cheerfulness that enriches his whole nature. It saddens him to think how unpleasantly Sarah is situated, and that he has not the power to snatch her from her uncongenial surroundings. He says he never before felt such a desire for wealth, and that he sometimes feels almost a disposition to murmur at the inequalities of fortune, which awards to some a portion of wealth they scarcely know what to do with, endows them with the means of dispensing happiness, and confers upon them numerous privileges, while so many, who seem to us, at least, not less deserving, are forced to drudge the vale of poverty, bearing not only our own burdens, which a manly heart could endure to do, but seeing those they love best suffer without the power to relieve them. This he said imparted the keenest suffering poverty could inflict.

He can not at present undertake the charge of a helpless wife, when he has already a feeble mother to support; and he does not wish to lose sight of the grand aim of his existence—to become a minister of the Gospel.

LITTLE ACTS AND GREAT PRINCIPLES.

I do n't know but I did a foolish thing to-day—a weak one. I have been trying to turn it over in my mind and determine its quality. Not that the act itself was of so very great importance, but the principle that governs our actions is always important, let the action be ever so trifling. The matter was this: Old Mr. Allen was going over to S. alone in a buggy. He is a very friendly old gentleman, and it occurred to him that perhaps I would like to ride over, and see my old friends there. This supposition was certainly true; for there are some people there whom it would give me great pleasure to see. Well, good Mr. Allen made the proposition to Frank, and he came with great alacrity to impart it to me, evidently thinking he was going to give me great pleasure; for he knows I have not been out much lately, and have drooped a little in consequence. The first thought that flashed into my mind when he told me of this opportunity was—O, unworthy!—"I have n't had a new thing since I came from there—I must wear the same old brown merino in which I appeared wherever I went the Winter I was there—the same black velvet bonnet, which was not *even then* new. And then my black silk—I have n't had it altered, and it is in the fashion of two or three years ago." And so I told Frank I thought I would n't go; and, as old Mr. Apsley says, I "*forewent*" the health-inspiring ride, and the greater invigorator—meeting valued friends—for a little foolish pride: perhaps it was; it looks that way to me now, holding the action up before me, and looking at it in the strong light of common-sense and conscience—for there really is a principle of duty involved in such actions. It is our duty to avail ourselves of social privileges—of means of health and cheerfulness when they are in our power, and we can use them with profit without conflicting with higher obligations. Frank could n't understand why I did n't go. Men never can understand these things—why should they? I never should have thought of telling him. Perhaps, though, it would have been better if I had; for my reasons (?), looking at them from his point of view, would have dwindled into insignificance—they would have wholly disappeared, I am thinking, like an illusion of the imagination. No wonder men think women inexplicable; they are so to themselves many times.

"DID N'T THINK," NO EXCUSE FOR NEGLECT OF DUTY.

Frank accused me to-day of being covetous. Perhaps I was; I own I did want something possessed by my neighbor. Possibly I indulged a little in a pharisaical spirit too; for I thought my neighbor does not obey the injunction, "Do to others," etc., as I would were our circumstances reversed.

The case was this: I do not feel strong yet,

and, lying on the lounge in the dining-room, through the window I saw Mrs. Wilkins's vines laden with rich clusters of purple grapes. I felt as though I wanted to stretch out my hand and pull some of them; I thought they would taste so good. I could not, like the fox, console myself with the thought that they were "*sour*," because beyond my reach. I knew they were sweet and luscious, as they looked tempting and beautiful. When Frank came in, I said, pointing to the vines, "Why can't Mrs. Wilkins send me a few bunches of those delicious grapes? She would never miss them; she has so many, and they would be so grateful and refreshing to me now, when I feel so weak and feverish."

"Why, you covetous little soul," he answered, "I suppose the woman has never thought of it—the groundwork probably of many of our omissions where the benefit of others is concerned."

"Well," I said, "but people *ought* to think, especially when they can afford pleasure to others without taking any from their own. It is certainly wrong *not* to think—as much wrong, according to my idea, as to *cause* unhappiness."

Just then father Braden came in, and Frank laughingly related to him that I had been coveting my neighbor's good things, and indulging in some uncharitable remarks upon their not bestowing them voluntarily — though I tried to prevent him.

"Well," said father Braden, with his usual outspokenness, "the little woman is right; and '*did n't think*' is no justification at all. It is the refuge behind which selfish people try to hide; but it only reveals them. If they cared much for the happiness of others, they *would* think, or, at least, they would learn to think. If we neglect to relieve misery when it is in our power, or to impart happiness when we can do so without sacrificing a disproportionate measure of our own, we are culpable for the misery we cause—amenable to higher laws than those of man."

"It is probable," said Frank, "that Mrs. Wilkins has never wanted for the luxuries, almost the necessaries of life; and as a general thing, we need to know deprivation ourselves to enable us to feel fully for that of others. Suffering is a wonderful quickener of the sympathies."

"That is just what I was thinking of," I said, "and I believe I have felt enough of it; so that when I see any one want for any thing I have, I shall wish to share it with them."

OUR DONATION PARTY.

We have had a *donation party,* one of those episodes in a minister's life, fraught with fear, and expectation, and hope, and anxiety, and sometimes followed by regrets as well as gratified feelings. It passed off as most such occasions do. We received some valuable and useful presents—some that I know were bestowed with a heart-warmth, and seemed to have a heart-fragrance about them, simple and homely though they might be. Many were showy, and, I felt, given more for show than from real feelings of friendship. Of this description was a costly crimson and gold annual, with the name of the giver ostentatiously inscribed on the fly-leaf. This, as Henry uncharitably said, would be a standing advertisement of the liberality of the *donor*, though the book was of very little value to the *donee*, who did not relish mawkish sentiment or sickly verses.

But gifts, of course, will partake something of the character of the giver, and will be showy or unobtrusive, directed to the needs or tastes of the receiver, or with an eye to appearances, accordingly. Directly after examining this expensive book, I took up a pair of warm, woolen stockings, soft and white, that good Mrs. Mowry had knitted for me with her own hands, and she so feeble and burdened with so many cares. I felt that these were indeed the widow's mite, and I could hardly avoid shedding tears as I held them in my hand. I told Frank I was sure they would warm me more than if they had been obtained in any other way. And they were to be trodden underfoot, hidden, like the good widow and her deeds, even while they blessed. But I said, "Though she and her good gifts are not appreciated here, they *will meet their reward.*"

I was interrupted by a call from Mrs. Marvin, and she had some unpleasant things to tell me—why do people want to be bearers of unpleasant news, when relating it does no good?—touching the donation party. Several persons were seriously offended, she said. I was surprised at this, for every thing had seemed to pass off with good feeling, and I expressed my surprise. She shook her head as though she thought I was not very far-seeing, and said there were some persons—some turbulent spirits—that always *would* be dissatisfied, let things be managed as they might; which is perhaps true enough. And I remembered how at S., on the occasion of an album-quilt party for me, a serious disaffection grew out of it, that was not healed when I left there.

Two very worthy sisters desired precedence in the matter, and because of the axiom, "Two bodies can not occupy the same space at the same time," ill feelings arose, both on the part of the one who obtained supremacy and the one that was defeated; and I remember the pleasure I should have felt from the gift, and the kindness that prompted its getting up by my neighbors, was nearly neutralized by the unpleasant circumstances attending its completion.

But the affair connected with the donation party was, that Mrs. Jenks thought Mrs. Mallory took too much upon herself in directing matters, which she did not think was her place, being comparatively a new-comer; and she—Mrs. Jenks—had always been accustomed to go ahead in such things ever since she had lived in the place—a good many years. Moreover, the said Mrs. Jenks thought that I seemed to favor the opposing faction; she had heard me consulting her about some arrangement on the evening of the party. She supposed it was because I thought Mrs. Mallory more stylish than she, when she had been so good a friend to us ever since we lived among them, and had done us so many favors, while Mrs. Mallory had scarcely lifted her finger, but must be called on to *direct*. She didn't think she could ever get over it, and she was sorry, for she had felt very friendly to us.

I was sorry too, not so much for the loss of her good services—for she *had* done us many a good turn—as the withdrawal of her good feeling. And to think that an innocent question of mine to Mrs. Mallory, who chanced to be nearest me when a little perplexity presented itself, should give rise to all this! "But what can't be cured must be endured." I thought, this is only another of our peculiar trials; for, of course, my inadvertency could not be explained away, or even referred to.

The other grievance arose with Mr. Delano and his wife, who had come several miles in the mud to attend the donation. They are good, well-meaning, old-fashioned Methodists, who think nothing ought to be changed to keep up with the times, even the cut of a garment. They thought there was entirely too much levity and show for the occasion, and that it was the minister's place to have checked it a little; but instead, they thought, he rather joined in and encouraged the hilarity—*he and his wife too!*

They were disappointed, for they had hitherto valued their pastor, and liked his sermons, and had been prepared to be pleased with his wife, but they thought her altogether too light for the station she occupied. And I had been trying to *simulate cheerfulness* on that evening, and to combat a sad and weary feeling that weighed me down, consequent upon my unusual labors for a few days to get things in readiness for the party, and the sad news contained in Sarah's letter. Ah, well! how prone we are to misjudge each other, and to misconstrue each other's actions! If I had acted *as I really felt*, then perhaps some one would have said that the minister's wife was uncordial and inhospitable, or haughty, or indifferent, or something of the kind.

Mrs. Marvin kindly expressed her fears that the disaffection on the part of Mr. and Mrs. Delano would result in their not coming to the village to Church any more, and withdrawing their support; for she said she thought, from something Mrs. Delano dropped in the course of conversation, she considered herself not treated with much attention on that evening; for that she had said I did not speak a half dozen words to her. Now, perhaps this rankled worst of all. And how *could* I, among that assembly of nearly one hundred and fifty people, extend particular attentions to all, wearied and confused as I felt, too? I endeavored to seek out all those who I thought would feel neglected if special attention were not shown them, and I remember thinking that night when I went tired to bed that I had succeeded.

CHAPTER VII.

PERSONS, OPINIONS, AND CRITICISMS.

MORRISON, OR BOTH KINDS OF LAZINESS.

MORRISON was in last evening. What a wreck he looks, in body and spirit, for a man scarcely past thirty! He has fine talents, a good heart, and is pleasing in person and deportment, but somehow he has *never got on well* in the world. Some one has said he always feels a peculiar respect for those who do not succeed in life, often finding them to possess sterling qualities. An idea obtains that dishonesty and intrigue are essential to advancement, because so many possessing these rise in the worldly scale—so many of the opposite character fail.

But I think, with father Braden, that the energy, perseverance, and tact more often found combined with these qualities are what carry one through, and that, coupled with honesty and integrity, they would achieve a higher success. Of course, conscientious scruples are not going to help thieves, pickpockets, and highwaymen to the accomplishment of their purposes, but they are not bars to success in an honest employment. The man of integrity often fails of his ends because he is not just to himself. He will take no unfair advantage of another, but often from an easy temper, lack of foresight, or an unwise trust, he allows the crafty and unscrupulous to take advantages that are rightfully his own, or which he might have gained.

But of Morrison and his failures. I think the most of them are caused by indolence of disposition, indecision, waiting for a favorable moment. He is not willing to break the shell of difficulty to obtain the kernel of success. He longs for position, wealth, power, but neglects the steps necessary to attain them. He was not born to these things; he does not seem qualified to achieve them, or at least does not put forth the power he possesses, and it is not at all probable that he will ever have them thrust upon him; so he must go on wishing, and longing, and vainly lamenting through life. He is the very puppet of circumstances, suffering himself to be driven hither and thither, stopped upon his course or sent backward by the very weakest of them when they are adverse, and I do not see that he avails himself of such as are favorable.

Some one has said, "Circumstances are the crutches of the helpless." They are certainly stumbling-blocks in the way of the weak when they do not favor their designs, though minds of the highest order overcome them, or make them stepping-stones to excellence and preferment. "A wise man tames difficulties as some tame wild beasts, making a lion embrace his keeper, a tiger kiss him, and an elephant kneel to him."

It is said there are two kinds of laziness—

one of the mind, and the other of the body. Poor Morrison, I fear, is afflicted with both; or, perhaps, it would be more charitable to call it that *vis inertiæ* which, it is said, usually accompanies genius. Father Braden talked very plainly to him. He did so from the interest he feels in him, and the desire he has that he shall assert himself a man. He thinks that Morrison possesses within himself the elements of success if he would but rouse himself, and throw off the shackles of irresolution that now bind his faculties in inaction. He might do much to gladden earth and people heaven, besides securing for himself that peace of mind which comes from doing one's life-work well, and which nothing else can bring. He suffers his mind to dwell upon the unfavorable circumstances of his condition—laments that he has no fortune, no influential friends to help him on—no father, no mother, no brother, no sister to aid him by sympathetic encouragements, as he fancies they would, without putting to use the talent given him—the power that in him dwells to carve his own way; and the longer he indulges the feebleness of irresolution, the weaker becomes his power of resistance. He is unhappy—discontented with himself and the world; he *feels* that he has not used faithfully the talents given him, and while he tries to blind his conviction of that by various sophistries, a sense of unworthiness "sits heavy at his heart." He looks wretched, haggard, worn, and weary of life, though scarcely past his first youth. How sad to see the young thus prematurely old! He needs "a wise, kind, firm friend—one who knows what he *ought* to do and *can* do, and who will make him do it." Do we not all, in some degree?

"My mind wants withing with bands of steel!" he said in relation to his vacillation of purpose. "Then is not adversity's 'iron hand' laid upon you for a wise purpose," I thought. "Should it not help you to concentrate your powers for some noble end?" Father Braden told him that he was suffering a kind of mental nightmare, which he might rise and shake off by a vigorous self-effort. It was a nightmare, he said, not only in the paralysis of his faculties, that held them chained, but in the imaginary "lion in the way" that prevented his advancement. "Review the last ten years of your life," he said to him, "and what obstacles can you see that have beset your path which energy and determination might not have removed? If you had chosen some useful pursuit, and resolutely followed it, what excellence might you have achieved by this time! Only think—ten years of onward march in one direction, even if you gain but a little at a time!—this is the way great results are attained in most cases. Your efforts are too intermittent, and you change your course too often to make any given point; and the longer you indulge these wavering habits, the stronger is their hold upon you—the weaker your self-confidence becomes!"

SHALL I TAKE LESSONS IN MUSIC AND FRENCH?

A widow lady, left without resources, except her own talents and acquirements, has lately come to the village. She proposes giving instruction in French, music, embroidery, etc., if she can obtain classes. I met her at Mrs. Atkins's. She seems a true lady, and I have no doubt is well versed in what she offers to teach. Mrs. Bates and Miss Harper called to-day, to see if I would not join some of the classes she is making up. Many of the married ladies were going to do so, they said. I felt a strong impulse to say "yes" at once; but I suppressed the inclination. I tried to turn the matter over in my mind, and resolve as would be best for me—best in every respect for the present and for the future.

I *do* try to adjust things right in this way—though perhaps self often shakes the balance. This time I resolved to put the case over for further consideration. I *did* covet a knowledge of French and music; I had a smattering of both, and had often wished to improve my slight acquisitions in these respects. Could I do so now without interfering with *platform duties?* I wanted to get Frank's opinion to help my decision; but I did n't like to ask him then lest they should think I was in leading-strings; so I told them I would think of it, and let them know. After they left I took counsel of the "powers that be"—superior in my own mind with regard to the matter. But before they could utter a word, Self-Conceit stepped boldly to the front, and spoke in a decided tone. "You possess more than an ordinary share of musical talent," he said. "You have a quick ear, a full, clear, rich voice. Have you not often been told so? Besides, when you took a few lessons on the piano, did not your teacher praise your delicacy and precision of touch, and say that you were capable of learning to play in a superior manner?"—and he appealed to Practical Sense for a confirmation of what he had said.

This staid personage did not contradict him, put down by his dogmatic manner, or wishing to be on the popular side.

"Music," he said, "is a real good. It is not merely to minister to sensual gratification—to give pleasure for an hour; but it has a harmonizing influence upon the temper, and is a potent allayer of murky spirits in the household."

And then came a whisper: "These accomplishments—French and music—will cause the minister's wife to be more looked up to—will increase her influence, confer a sort of superiority upon her which will better fit her for her position."

I think it was Vanity that put in this plea. Though he disguised his voice a little, I recognized his style of sentiment; and I was glad I detected him, or I might have given undue weight to the suggestions of the insinuating changeling. After these upstarts had subsided, plain Common-Sense and Prudence came forward, and spoke slowly and calmly. The matter is very clear and easy to decide, they both agreed, if viewed in the right light.

"You have about sixteen hours per diem in which to discharge the duties that devolve upon you as a wife—a pastor's wife, a member of society, a housekeeper, etc.; make an estimate of the time they ought to consume, reserving something for contingencies, and see if you have room in your life at present to gain a knowledge of the accomplishments you covet."

I listened to this dictation, and came to the conclusion that for *me*, at present, to attempt this would bring a discord into my life instead of introducing a fresh element of harmony. So I tried to contract my desires within the sphere of my present circumstances. The time may come when I may be permitted to enlarge their boundaries without sacrificing the greater to the less—a mistake to which we are all so blindly, weakly prone, and which I must try not to fall into.

ALLSTON, OR THE SELFISH STUDENT.

I think it wrong for any one to live a mere student life, like Allston, our neighbor. What if he does possess wealth that places him above the necessity of laboring for a livelihood? Every one ought to pay something for living in the world. Now, I can't see that Allston does this. To be sure he is a fine, gentlemanly man, courteous to those he meets, and minds his own business. But he lives in almost monkish seclusion, buried among his books, which he studies merely for his own gratification; not to gather from them wisdom to regulate his own life that he may bless the world by an example of a perfect man, or as nearly so as our frail humanity will admit, nor to garner up knowledge to scatter abroad for the benefit of others. He seems to have no such aims, but to think, that so long as he does not interfere with the happiness of others he has a right to spend his time as it pleases him.

But should the leisure, talent, and wealth that has fallen to his share be used only to subserve his individual pleasure? It is plainly wrong to spend it thus; and as plainly, it appears to me, he misses all the glory of life by so devoting it.

But he does not know how great is his loss! His books—though he lives, moves, and breathes by them—have not taught him this precious life-lesson, that it is not good for man to live for himself alone. Surrounded by every luxury, and with the means of ministering to every selfish desire, he has yet a dissatisfied look. There is not in his appearance half the fullness of content and relish of life that is seen in that of his neighbor, O'Donigan, who saws wood for his daily bread. He lives up to the highest requirements of his nature. The fastidious, self-indulgent Mr. Allston does not. There are deeps in his nature that have never been stirred — wants and longings that have never been satisfied.

To be sure he has no wife nor children to soothe his lonely hours, or to vex his social and busy ones; but it is not this. There is a mine of deep enjoyment where he might delve for treasure; but he only picks pebbles from the surface. He might make for himself objects of interest and pursuit that would leave no barren spots in his life. How meager is it now, with all its aims centered upon the little point of self! The less right has he to lead this selfish life that he has never earned the means of luxury and ease he uses, for his wealth was inherited.

CAUGHT IN A BAD PLIGHT.

"My banker," says some one, "always makes a low bow to my new coat, a moderate one to my old." I was reminded of this to-day by Mrs. Allen's treatment of me. I did not feel very well, and looked about as much out of sorts as I felt—was *en deshabille* both in dress and in spirit—disheveled in *air* as well as in *hair*—down at the heel literally and figuratively: correspondences not unusual with me, I fear. In this state of things, preparing to mix some gingerbread, I found my ginger was *minus*, and had no one to send for more. Frank is very fond of gingerbread. I had promised to have some with tea; so I put on my sunbonnet, and thought I would go in to Mrs. Allen's, just across the garden, and ask her to lend me a little. I took a tea-cup, and ran in, in the familiar way I am used to, but was taken quite aback at seeing two stylish-looking ladies seated in the dining-room, robed in fashionable *negligés*, and *doing* some embroidery, or other lady-like trifle. Mrs. Allen was not in the room, and we—the visitors and I—stared at each other mutually for the space of a few minutes, no doubt about equally surprised—I to see a couple of fine ladies where I had expected to find only good old Mrs. Allen in her blue-check apron, and they, doubtless, to see such a disarrayed figure as I presented burst in, cup in hand, and then stand staring as if turned to stone. I am sure they could not, by any possibility, have mistaken me for a celestial cup-bearer; yet had one suddenly appeared before them, they could scarcely have looked more astonished. Luckily Mrs. Allen came in to break the spell; though she, too, seemed not a little surprised to see me standing there in that trim; but she recovered herself, and introduced me to the Misses Grey, her nieces from M. "Mrs. Edmonds," she said, in presenting me— hesitating before adding, "*our minister's wife*," which she is wont to pronounce with a peculiar unction when I am *dressed up*, and a triumphant air, as if she was proud of me. "It's my dress," I said to myself, "that the old lady is ashamed of." And when I saw the supercilious looks of the young ladies, I said, "They are due to my dress."

BROCKWAY, OR THE DOWNWARD CAREER.

I was thinking of James Brockway this evening, and I thought, "O, how sad it is to see the human form divine marred, and its Maker's image gradually defaced by the influence of evil passions! How sadder still that the soul is scarred and deformed by the same process!" I seem to see before me now James as he looked and was when a boy of ten—of noble, frank, and intelligent countenance; generous, chivalric, and truthful in disposition; kind and sympathetic in feeling. About this time his mother died; his father had died some years before. He went to live with a cousin, who treated him unkindly, and spoiled his temper by incessant irritation and fault-finding. James had not been used to this, for his mother had always been kind and gentle in her manner toward her children.

This woman made him so unhappy—not being willing to afford him any enjoyment, even when it did not conflict with her own interest or convenience—that he left her, ran away, and, falling in with some low fellows who were rafting on the river—one of whom had formerly lived in his own village and enticed him—he joined them for a trifling sum, which they agreed to pay him for assisting about cooking their food, and performing some other little services. He went with them a few seasons, and in that time had taken several degrees in vice. He was initiated into the mysteries of gambling; could smoke and chew tobacco with an air, and roll out an oath with as much nonchalance as any rowdy of them all.

I saw him when he came home to B., after leaving these unprofitable companions, and what a change there was in him! He had a leering, impudent look, a swaggering air, rolled in his gait, and seemed altogether unlike the sprightly, gentlemanly boy I had known a few years before.

The transition from the rigid rule of his cousin to the reckless freedom of the life of those unscrupulous boatmen, who feared neither God nor man, was too much for his yielding nature, before undisciplined and untried in the furnace of temptation. He fell readily into their lawless ways and habits. Every tendency to evil in his nature was brought out and strengthened by their example and enticements, while the good which, under his mother's wise and gentle influence, had marked his character, became deadened from disuse.

Three years more and I saw him again. This was when we lived at S. He was then a stout lad of eighteen, and all the revolting traits that had begun to take precedence in his character at fifteen had stronger hold, and seemed a part of his nature; they were confirmed, and swayed not only his actions, but marked his expression and controlled his motions. I could scarcely discern a trace in any of them of the noble spirit which had once actuated him. Occasional drunkenness was added to his other bad habits, and its effects were visible in the bloated countenance, the stupid look, and the thickness of utterance which clings to some drunkards even when they are sober.

How sad it made me to look at him when he called to see me for old acquaintance' sake—for we had been schoolmates, although I was some years his senior—and how I wished I could present to him a picture of himself as he had been at ten, and exhort him for the memory of the mother who had loved him so, and which he still cherished—for tears, hardened though he was, sprang to his eyes when I spoke of her—how I wished to present this picture to him, and exhort him to strive to regain the excellence it represented, and which she had so carefully nurtured! How I wished a remembrance of this good and gentle being might prove a talisman to rouse the sparks of goodness which, I felt, were still latent in his nature—far, far down beneath the rubbish and filth of sin that had gathered above, but I hoped not quite extinguished them! But I had not courage to make the experiment. He was beyond my influence, I thought, wedded to his evil habits, and any thing I could say with a view to benefit him would be derided as preaching, and made a jest of among his low companions. Perhaps I was wrong—I feel now that I was—but I shrank from the task, refraining from sowing good seed because the soil seemed unpromising.

Who knows but some kindly admonition from my lips might have taken root in his heart, and sprung up, and been productive of good to this seemingly-abandoned soul? We should never withhold our hand because good results from our efforts seem uncertain. We ought to do our duty and leave the event with Heaven. How many times I have had occasion to reproach myself with a neglect of this kind! It was so in those days; it is so now. When shall I ever learn promptness in the way of my duty, and not let vain scruples or false delicacy turn me aside, or make me hesitate till the occasion is past?

My sins of *omission* of every sort weigh upon me heavily; and to omit to do good, when it is in my power, is as culpable as to commit actual wrong. How much more noble to assist feeble resolutions to amend the life, or to plant in the soul the seeds of good resolves, that may spring up and bear fruit to eternal life, than to "cause two blades of grass to grow where but one grew before!" Yet we neglect these weightier matters, and give the stress of our endeavors to the outward and perishing.

SOON TO BE ON THE WING AGAIN.

Only three months more and we must be on the wing again. I do sometimes a little dread the idea of *breaking up new ground*—making new acquaintances—but the ordeal is not so formidable to me as it once was. I shall be truly sorry to leave my friends here—those whom I have found genuinely such, in deed, and in word, and in the manifestation of sympathy in every possible way. How happy they have made me! for I think one of the greatest blessings of life springs from genuine friendly intercourse.

To be sure, as Henry says, I expect to find some friends in every post; still I never feel inclined to change the old for the new. I never can attain the facility possessed by some, who, "when far away from the friends that they love, have but to make love to the lips that are near."

I think, if I were inclined to envy the condition of any class of people, it would be that of the farmer, owning the land of his fathers and dwelling upon it. It would be so pleasant, I should think, to live all one's life in one spot, and to have it endeared by a thousand associations that must meet us on every hand—the animals we have reared, and that show us affectionate recognition; the grounds we have beautified; the trees we have planted; and perhaps the graves of our loved ones. Then how much more secure and independent one would feel when his reliance was, as Franklin says, "upon the blessing of God and his own industry," instead of the tide of popular favor, as is the case with some of the professions. Next to the way of life I have chosen, I would prefer that of the farmer.

And, speaking about modes of life, how often people mistake, I think, in influencing the natural bias of their children's inclinations, and choosing for them occupations and professions for which they are unsuited by the original constitution of their minds! I have seen a striking instance of this lately.

Mr. Luther has two sons. The elder is a delicate, sensitive young man, poetically inclined, I should say—at any rate, of the poetic temperament, whether his feelings ever express themselves in poetry or not. He is fond of solitude and contemplation, though gay and cheerful in congenial society. On account of his studious habits and somewhat slender constitution, his parents have decided upon the profession of the law for him. Now, it seems to me just the thing for which he is peculiarly unfitted. Contact with busy life, compulsive toil, the dry details and tedious sinuosities of the law would be continually distasteful to him, and he must wrench and distort his nature to render them endurable. A few acres of land to till, with plenty of books to read in the intervals of toil—companionship of his own choosing—and his days might glide peacefully and happily away. There are those who love the bustle, and the turmoil, and the strife of business. Let them be left for such.

MORAL LAW A REALITY.

I have been reading Wayland's Moral Science. He says, "If it shall be found I have thrown any light whatever upon *the science of human duty*, I shall have cause for gratitude." He has done so for me. I believe I should have been a better woman if I had read it years ago. And how much ignorance there is of this science, and what misery springs from it! Is it not this that swells "every day's report of wrong and outrage with which earth is filled"—makes "lands intersected by a narrow frith abhor each other," as well as causes those small bickerings and strifes, those envyings and enmities that so often disturb the harmony of social and domestic life—this ignorance of our duty to ourselves, our neighbor, and humanity at large? People do not clearly see that their shortcomings in duty toward themselves or others entail evil consequences, or involve a loss of something that might have been enjoyed if they had acted up to the highest law of right. Wayland says, "There is an order of sequence in morals just as invariable as in physics. Certain moral acts are followed by certain moral consequences which can not be eluded or averted; yet, because they are not always immediate or as plainly to be seen as the consequences of physical actions, men hope to elude or escape them—do not believe in their existence, perhaps, or have never given a thought to the matter; yet the result is just as certain as that if you put your hand in the fire it will be burned. This law, Arthur explains thus: "There is a law governing in the affairs of men, with its award of good and evil, according to the term of every one's obedience or disregard thereto. Ignorance of this law exempts no one from punishment; yet four-fifths of the human family are entirely unconscious of its existence. This is the law of action and reaction. Every thing we do affects ourselves or others in some way, for there can not be such a thing as an act without an effect proportional to the action. The importance of a life in obedience to this law must be seen. We see and acknowledge this with regard to great matters, but in *little things*, as they are called, where no violation of penal statutes or public opinion occurs, we imagine that none exists. But this is an error; for there is no act of our lives, good or bad, little or great, but sooner or later will react upon us with its full quota of consequences."

CHAPTER VIII.

MADE UP OF VARIETIES.

MRS. MASSON, OR DISORDER AND APOLOGIES.

I DO N'T know that I ever realized more vividly the importance of neatness and order than to-day, when I saw such a lamentable instance of the lack of them. I hope I shall learn a lesson by it—keep a sharper look-out for failures in these respects in myself; though I do not wish to give these very desirable qualities too great prominence, so that they shall overrun and trample down larger virtues.

Sometimes efforts to secure physical order produce much moral disorder by the ill-temper they cause, which is a sin as well as a very unpleasant social and domestic quality. But about this instance that came under my eye: I went to call on Mrs. Masson, the presiding elder's wife. I ought to have done so before, but home cares have prevented. She met me at the door, and I am afraid my countenance showed how much surprised I was at the appearance she presented; for she began making apologies about her dress as she showed me the way to the parlor, and continued them while she was taking my things, as if this was the only time in her life that she had ever offended against neatness, and present appearances had been brought about by some unavoidable combination of circumstances, and caused the unusual phenomenon which I could not avoid noticing.

It is easy, however, to discriminate between an accidental careless state of the dress—which sometimes, I grant, *will* occur to the best regulated in this respect—and one that is indigenous, as I readily perceived it was in the present instance. I'm afraid I have n't patience and charity enough for these people; but it seems to me that their elaborate excuses show a mental state as slip-shod and ill-regulated as their apparel and surroundings.

Every thing in Mrs. Masson's house that came under my notice—and I could not help seeing, disorder was so glaring—every thing confirmed the impression the dress of the mistress had made upon me when she presented herself at the door; and I could scarcely help smiling at the profuse apologies upon the *accidental* state of things, which I have no doubt were made in good faith—so blind are we to errors in ourselves which are plainly apparent to all others; and when our attention is directed to them by our consciousness of the observation of others, we fancy we only err *occasionally* in that way, and that it is not the permanent condition of things. This may be, perhaps, because often we are not at heart, from principle and choice, or the natural bent of our tastes, what we have *become* from habit formed by controlling circumstances, and of the strength of which we are not conscious because we are all right at the center. It is for this reason, perhaps, that we often hear people speak of errors of conduct in others which are glaring in themselves.

I remember reading about a phrenologist visiting an alms-house, and examining the head of a little girl; he remarked that she had a large development of order.

"No," the matron said; "she has given us a great deal of trouble by the lack of it— more than any one in the establishment."

"Nevertheless," the phrenologist said, "she possesses the faculty in a striking degree;" and from that time it developed itself till she became the most orderly member of the institution. From what did the change spring? From encouragement; from which arose a new-born hope and belief that she could be orderly by self-effort. Had her extreme faultiness in this respect arisen from too much blame, inducing a conviction that she could not be other than she was? I believe many are confirmed in wrong courses by having their faults continually brought before them—"by repetition hammered on the ear," that they feel it is useless trying to reform.

These thoughts ran through my mind while I sat in the parlor, waiting for Mrs. Masson to make some change in her dress—as she had begged a few moments to do—and looked round at the evidences of carelessness that every-where met my eye. I wondered if the defaced pictures, torn annuals, and daguerreotypes *off the hinges* that covered the table were the work of a day!—the soiled carpet and curtains, and the looking-glass so bespeckled by vagrant flies, and begreased by bread-and-butter fingers, that I scarcely knew my own image reflected in it!

And the dirty-faced, tangle-locked little girl, with one pantalet torn off just below the knee and the other hanging in tatters about her begrimed ankle—I wondered if that same accident had brought about these things just at that time, or was it a remarkable coincidence! And the manners of the little girl, too, seemed in no better trim than her dress; for when I spoke to her she stared at me a moment without answering, and then ran away with her fingers in her mouth, casting furtive glances back over her shoulder.

I should have been glad to believe that this specimen of manners, or rather of want of manners, was only the effect of a passing mood of the child; but I sadly feared that, like the rest I saw, it was the *normal state of things*. I feared, because I feel interested in Mrs. Masson and her excellent husband, and I know that these things are drawbacks upon their usefulness and influence. Surely dress—the appointments of a house, *do* exert a serious influence, not only upon our own self-respect, but the regard in which we are viewed by others; and when they are untidy—even filthy—they certainly must lower us in both.

"By others' faults the wise correct their own."

EMPLOYMENT FOR ALL THE FACULTIES.

How much of the unhappiness that exists in the world arises from a lack of sufficient employment for all the faculties, or of occupation suited to the character of the mind; and how many mistakes with regard to the latter are made by parents and guardians, and even by those who choose their life-work for themselves! The inclination should be consulted in these things, as well as fitness, and perhaps it will be found that they usually go together if left unbiased. We are more likely to excel in what suits us, and perform it with greater ease.

"The toil we hate fatigues us soon."

Those who have nothing to do, or rather who do nothing, are often looked upon by the overtasked as peculiarly fortunate; but we can have no fullness of enjoyment unless all our faculties are brought into action, all exercised in a due degree, though our existence may be a sort of negative state, in which we experience neither pain nor positive pleasure. "A dead calm," says some one, "settles over the person who leads an idle life." Many suffer from this vacuity, are restless, dissatisfied with themselves and all around them, and know not why.

Many women especially, whose circumstances prevent the necessity of their taking part in their domestic affairs, or who perhaps consider it ungenteel to do so, and who lack mental resources, often suffer from illness of both body and mind, and are all unwitting of the cause. Misfortunes would often prove a blessing, and might not unfrequently arouse them to activity. I have seen instances wherein this was verified.

But this peevishness, restlessness, nervousness — which is sometimes only another term for ill-temper—whatever you may term it, is to be distinguished from the unhappiness that arises from delicacy of organization, which sometimes causes its possessors to be dissatisfied with things around them, and to be susceptible of exquisite pain from causes that would not be noticed by those of coarser fiber. They are not able themselves perhaps to analyze the cause of the uneasiness; they feel hurt when the delicate chords of their spirits are jarred by the imperfections in the persons and things around them, as a fine musical ear is hurt by the jar of a false note in music; nor are they generally understood by others, and the expression of their dissatisfaction is often called ill-nature, attributed to a fault-finding spirit. Children of this temperament are often made what they are thought to be by the treatment they receive.

Smellie has said that "no sentient being, with mental powers greatly superior to those of man, could possibly live and be happy in this world. The misery of such a being would be very great. With senses more delicate and refined, with perceptions more acute and penetrating, with a taste so exquisite that the objects around him would by no means gratify it, he must be born only to be miserable. Even in our present condition, the sameness and insipidity of objects and pursuits, the futility of pleasure, and the infinite sources of excruciating pain, are supported with great difficulty by cultivated and refined minds. Increase our sensibility, continue the same objects and pursuits, and no one could bear to live."

Now, there are those so finely constituted as to suffer, in a great degree, what Smellie supposes of the imaginary being he has drawn: those of the *poetic temperament*, as it is called, who can be happy only in a sphere of beauty and harmony—those, "the lyre of whose souls should be fanned only by airs of Eden, and give out its music in a heavenly clime." There *are* such. How they are jarred by the discords of life! Children of this temperament are often confirmed in irritability of temper by injudicious treatment, and instead of diffusing joy around them, as it is their mission to do, become scourges to their friends and society. They should have gentle treatment, and interesting employment sufficient for activity of body and mind, interchanged with amusement. Idleness, vacuity of mind, will increase the susceptibility to outward impressions that causes them so much pain; *harshness will put a finer edge upon their already too keen sensibilities.*

SELF-KNOWLEDGE.

How little we know of the mechanism of these bodies of ours! How little of the constitution of our minds! How ignorant we are of the causes that derange their delicate machinery, causing our actions to be inharmonious — our lives to swerve aside from the great end of being!

Is n't it wonderful that men will roam among the stars in search of knowledge when they neglect to look into themselves? Ah, true enough, "what shadows we are and what shadows we pursue!"

"Know thyself," is a precept descended from Heaven,
Which to weak, erring man for his guidance was given;

Yet he heeds not its teaching, but stretches afar
His vision to scan distant planet and star.
Caves, cataracts, rivers, he rushes to view,
Ransacking for novelties Old World and New;
The pyramids mounts, and afar sends his eye,
And climbs Chimborazo fresh wonders to spy;
He travels to China to scale its grand wall;
Yet he knows not himself—greatest wonder of all!

It is this lack of self-knowledge that gives reality to this sad picture:

Men will wrangle for religion,
  And for it their lives will give;
Write and fight to help maintain it—
  Any thing but rightly live.

CROW-BAR DIGNITY.

What false notions some people have of dignity! Dignity is the result of true superiority and self-respect; and what a ludicrous caricature of it is sometimes presented by that touch-me-not air which some persons endeavor to assume, under the delusion that it constitutes dignity! "Crow-bar dignity," as some one has styled it, "a mysterious carriage of the body, put on to cover some defect of the mind." Genuine dignity is a well-fitting garment, easily worn and pliant to the touch; the other is a porcupine affair, bristling at every point, and worn with labor.

A WASTED AND BARREN LIFE.

I was interrupted by a call from Mrs. Bennett and her daughter Eva, a little girl of ten years. Mrs. Bennett was an acquaintance of my girl days, but I should scarcely have recognized the demure, bashful little maiden she was then in the showy, bedizened, self-assured woman of the world into which she is metamorphosed. "How she is improved since she went to the city!" I have heard people say. To me she is just the reverse.

Mr. Bennett, when she married him, was a city clerk, who saw her when she was visiting an aunt in the city, and fell in love with her red cheeks. He has a wholesale establishment of his own now, and is quite wealthy. They board at a fashionable hotel, and there her child was born and has been reared thus far.

How sad it is, I think, to bring up a child in such a place! Poor thing! No home influences to foster those womanly graces that can thrive properly in no other atmosphere! And she seems as vain and artificial as her surroundings have been. She is pretty, but the false life she has led has effaced all genuine child-grace from her manner, and from her mind, too, I fear. I wondered her mother could not see this, for she was brought up simply, and had a heart once, but the false life to which her husband's wealth has introduced her has, I fear, made her lose her relish for truth and simplicity.

After they were gone, father Braden, who was present, remarked that frivolity and indolence usually divided the time of hotel-dwellers—ladies—though they *might* find useful employment for their time even there, where there were no home duties to engross them. Dressing, eating, lounging with some trumpery book, shopping, exchanging calls of ceremony with those as idle and frivolous as themselves, frequenting crowds where laborious efforts were made to secure pleasure, actuated by no desire of self-improvement except in the art of dressing and outward accomplishments, no endeavors for the good of others—what a wasted, barren existence!

"Do you ever expect to get to heaven from this place?" asked Bishop Chase of a lady who had spent a large part of her life in a hotel; and well the query and the doubt it suggested.

UNEXPECTED AND UNTIMELY VISITORS.

I fear I was a little unreasonable to-day, and made Frank feel unpleasantly. I must confess that I was somewhat out of humor, pettish, irritable, the result, I suppose, of my feeling tired and unwell, though I do n't think this ought to excuse the mood I was in. My reason should rule, and check this waywardness, and not suffer it to make myself and others unhappy. It was the old story that housekeepers have suffered from the beginning, I suppose—people coming unexpectedly when I was unprepared to receive them in my household arrangements, and felt too wearied in mind and body to take up cheerfully the task. To *me* it is a task, under such circumstances, of making myself agreeable.

It was Mrs. Mason and her three children, who called to stay while her husband got his horses shod at the blacksmith shop in the village, and transacted some other business. I knew she would stay to tea, and while I was taking her things I thought, "I have not a mouthful of sugar in the house;" and what housewife thinks of getting tea for visitors without the inevitable cake, which, after all, is more for show than any thing else half the time, and leaves the table untouched or scarcely tasted; still it is considered indispensable for filling up, and I knew Mrs. Mason regarded it so. Frank had been so much interrupted during the week that he was behind in preparing his sermon; and I know if he is interrupted in a train of thought — thrown off the track — it is difficult for him to resume it again; so I felt reluctant to call him down to go of errands. I had intended, when Henry came in from his school, to ask him to get some things that were needed, but that would be too late for Mrs. Mason's tea.

How these little things vex us sometimes when we feel weary in mind and body—much more than they ought to be allowed to do! I had just got every thing arranged for Sunday, and I knew from experience that Mrs. Mason's children would leave the prints of their fingers not only on my clean chintz lounge-cover and cushions, upon which they left marks at their last visit—for they always want bread and butter to "*stay their stomachs*" for tea—and that the room I had just put in such nice order would be disarranged generally. I feared more especially for my white muslin curtains that I had just finished hanging at the parlor windows, and which had given me so much trouble to clear-starch and iron.

It turned out according to my apprehensions; for not only was my lounge daubed and disarranged, but a book of prints that Henry presented me at Christmas had some of its most beautiful pictures disfigured by their unruly fingers; besides, in quarreling for the possession of it, they got tangled up in my curtains, behind which the boy ran for the safe-keeping of his prize, and a large cross-rent, which I despair of ever darning, was left behind as a mark of his prowess. My poor geranium, too, that I have nursed so tenderly, apportioning it the sunlight in due season, and taking care that "the winds of heaven visit it not too roughly," was plucked nearly bare by their lawless hands.

And their mother sat looking on as placid as if "the dear little things," as she calls them, were amusing themselves in the most harmless manner possible; at least she did so till the curtain catastrophe, when she administered a shower of cuffs upon the offender, upon which he sent up a shrill cry that rent my ears more intolerably than his fingers had rent my curtains. Now, of course, I must preserve my serenity under these circumstances, and I know that I ought to have done it, but I must confess I found it exceedingly difficult to do so. I felt strongly inclined to *beat an accompaniment* upon the urchin's ears to the raps his mother was bestowing, but I restrained this inclination, of course, and tried to say it was no matter, though I imagine not very gracefully.

The last scene in the drama was enacted at the supper-table. I suppose I shall smile ten years hence, when I look on this record, to think how seriously annoyed I allowed myself to be, and how I could scarcely keep the tears of vexation from welling up in my eyes and running over. During the whole time of supper the children were clamoring vociferously for every thing upon the table; devouring what fell into their hands as ravenously as so many famished young animals; executing diagrams with the juice of my stewed plums upon the white table-cloth I had ironed with so much care; and lifting up, with their fingers dripping with butter, to their mouths the hot griddle-cakes that I had substituted for the stirred-cake which I *should* have made but for the default of sugar.

After they had gone I sat down and cried—I couldn't help it. Such a closing up, I thought, of my day of toil, which I had *intended* to round off reading a pleasant book Mrs. Allen had sent me, and the anticipation of which had buoyed me up all day, and helped to make my labor light.

FRANK'S REMONSTRANCE.

Frank came in and found me in tears, and tenderly inquired the cause. I hardly know what I said, but I know it was something unbecoming my position and character, and which was made worse by the fact that poor Frank has vexations enough—trials enough without my increasing their burden by my querulous complaining. I felt condemned when I saw the sad look that came to his face as he listened to me; and when he spoke a few words of kind remonstrance I could have thrown myself in his arms, and asked forgiveness for the clouds which my pettishness so often brings to our domestic sky; but a little remnant of the old Eve was still at bottom, and restrained me, and he returned to his study with his spirits depressed by my selfishness in troubling him with a relation of my domestic grievances, which I should have withheld, at least for the present. I hear him pacing up and down in his study now, as he is in the habit of doing when he is disturbed in mind. Shall I go up and tranquilize him by a sight of the serenity I have attained?—for the nap I took on the lounge, after clearing away my tea-things, and this recording of my trials—which always seems like an outpouring into the ear of some sympathetic friend—have made me myself again; and the vexations of the day, which assumed such formidable proportions before, to dwindle to an almost indistinguishable point. I seem to view them from a great distance, or look upon them as having occurred to another. I see them through the other end of the telescope. May I be enabled to reverse it oftener! Goodnight.

SCRAPS ABOUT PERSONS AND THINGS.

Moral purity is as essential to the wellbeing of the mind as personal cleanliness is to the health of the body, and the condition of each reacts upon the other.

> "Even from the body's purity, the mind
> Receives a secret, sympathetic aid;"

and a well-regulated mind is necessary to the highest degree of physical health.

Mr. Congden is emphatically a dry speaker. Possessing the imaginative faculty in a high degree, he ignores imagination—a due exercise of which would enable him to drape his thoughts with beauty and variety—presenting naked facts, bare and skeleton-like abstractions. With a nature eminently social, that *needs* "social friction" to elicit mental electricity—which would give force and vividness to his thoughts, and relieve his style of the dullness and somberness which are its prevailing characteristics—he denies himself social pleasures. Thus, endowed naturally with intellectual vigor, activity, grace, all of which might be increased by exercise, he turns himself into a mental Fakir, giving no variety of play to his faculties; and the productions of his mind lack color and vitality accordingly. Shall we, "with blind presumption bold," endeavor to be wiser than He who has "strung the great harp of existence with all its wild, and wonderful, and manifold chords?"

The constant watchfulness that must be exercised to *hide* our faults, requires more self-denial than would suffice to rid ourselves of them.

My heart yearns toward the neglected and unfortunate, even though they be guilty. Why should we spurn from us those who have been led into error? Are we without blame ourselves? Weakness may have caused it, or blind and unknowing they may have taken the path of wrong. Who can tell the pangs of remorse they suffer? We know not how easily they might, if taken kindly by the hand, be led back to the right path, and restored to happiness! And shall we, by the severity with which we treat them, drive them further into vice and misery? — passing them by with an air that seems to say, "I am more holy than thou," when, perhaps, in the eyes of Him to whom all hearts and motives are laid bare they are less guilty than ourselves.

The more I become enlightened upon the subject of health, the more I am astonished at the ignorance that prevails with regard to it, and the means of promoting—of increasing it. How blind I have been in these respects—how I have erred! Now I see others violating its foundation rules in the same manner I have done.

It may be said emphatically—not irreverently—with regard to this matter, "We have done those things that we ought not to have done, we have left undone those things that we ought to have done, and *there is no health in us*"—health of body, or health of soul. How we fail!

CHAPTER IX.

EXPERIENCES OF A SICK HOUSEKEEPER.

CHILLS AND FEVER.

THE station, M., to which we were this year assigned, is in an ague district, and we had not been here long before I began to feel bilious symptoms. I suppose my system happened to be in the right state to be readily influenced by the climate, for I had not been well for some time before. I had a dull pain in my head—felt weary and listless by day, and feverish and restless of nights. Frank, raking up some of his medical knowledge, prescribed Seidlitz powders to subdue my feverishness—told me to keep quiet and not get fatigued, and he thought I would get well in a few days.

This was Saturday evening. I had never taken any of these powders before, but they were very cooling and refreshing, and grateful to the taste, and I thought them quite a luxury, and told Frank-I did not doubt I should get along without any other medicine, my head was so much better, and my fever subdued.

Sunday morning was cool and misty, and I did not think it best to go out to Church. After fixing Frank off, I felt a little tired, and a feverish thirst. I bethought me of my cooling powders. The box containing them stood on a stand before the window of my bedroom, which was open a little. I mixed one, and drank it. It was delicious. I shall never forget the sensation of delightful coolness it diffused through my frame. I craved another, reasoning, perhaps, like the Irishman, who thought if one pill would benefit him, the whole box would do so in the same proportion. So I mixed another, and raised it to my lips. Before I had finished swallowing it, the hand that held the glass turned icy cold. I set it down. "The air from the window is too chill this morning," I thought, and I closed it. *Both* hands were cold!—a chilly sensation began to creep up my back. I looked at my nails. The blood was huddled up at the roots of them in a purple cloud. "*It is the ague!*" I exclaimed. Chills were running all over me.

I took a comforter from the closet, and, lying down upon the bed, I covered myself with it, to shake at my leisure. I lay—I do n't know how long—with that mortal coldness upon me. It passed away by degrees, and a burning heat ensued. I threw the bed-clothes from me. I was parched with intolerable thirst; I crept to the stand, where there was some water left in the pitcher—I say crept, for I really felt weak and exhausted from the muscular exertion through which my unseen enemy had put me. I could not swallow the water; it was warm and nauseous to my taste. I dared not go to the well, for I was not sufficiently acquainted with the disease to know whether it would be safe for me to do so in my feverish state; besides, there was no water drawn. I remembered that I had turned it all into the pitcher to prepare my powders, and I did not feel strong enough to draw up the bucket.

I took a pillow from the bed and a comforter, and throwing them on the carpet, lay down upon them in quiet resignation to my fate. How slowly the hands of the little clock in our room went round! They scarcely seemed to move at all. Its tickings did not half keep pace with the throbbings of my aching temples. Frank would not be home till four. "What an age!" I thought. I had never felt the burning of fever in my veins before. My brain began to be excited, and my thoughts ran into blank verse. Wild they reveled over heaven and earth!—sometimes wound up to the highest pitch of ecstasy, again assuming the plaintive wail of despair.

I have wished sometimes I could have preserved these fever-born fancies; but they passed away as my brain cooled. Then I began counting—the flowers upon the paper, the panes of glass in the window—every thing; wearing my brain going over and over with it, but seeming unable to avoid it; and then I fell to *tracing constellations* among the flies grouped upon the ceiling.

The time *did* wear away, and at last—O, joy!—I heard Frank's step coming up the walk. How my heart beat when I heard his hand on the latch! "I do n't believe a weary prisoner ever felt greater gladness when he heard the footsteps of one who was to liberate him approach his dreary dungeon, and heard the welcome key grate in the rusty lock!" I said to myself when I heard him approaching. The door of the room where I lay was open into the hall, and I shall never forget his look of blank dismay as he saw me lying there, with the traces of fever still burning on my cheeks, a livid ring around my lips, and wild, dilated eyes. This, he afterward told me, was the appearance I presented when his eyes fell upon me. I had borne up well till

I saw him; then I wept like a child. I must *drop the curtain* here upon this scene, for Frank does not like to have his tenderness the subject of remark.

ABOUT A DOCTOR AND A NURSE.

I feel the need of some amusement. I am very lonely sometimes; so I will jot down something about my nurse, though, indeed, sometimes I am almost as much disposed to cry as laugh over it. I would not wish to deride or disparage the good woman who acted in that capacity during some part of my illness; but I shall do her no injury by portraying some of her peculiarities, while we may derive amusement from it.

When I had a chill on Sunday Frank was in great consternation, feared I was going to be seriously ill, and proposed at once sending for Dr. Wanzer, the only regular physician in the place, and he one of those who administer *calomel* in all cases, from a tumble down stairs—

it is *said* he actually *did* give calomel to a boy in such a case—to an attack of fever. I could not think of having him; I thought I would rather trust to the disease; but to have the disease and a course of remedies from him to combat at the same time I was afraid would be too much for nature. Frank had no more faith in him than I, but it is so natural, when one is sick, to catch at the veriest straw in the way of a doctor, though we deride and express our unbelief in them when well.

> "This is the way physicians mend us—
> *Secundum artem.* But although we sneer
> In health, when sick we call them to attend us."

Well, it was settled that I need not have Dr. Wanzer, as the idea seemed to give me so much uneasiness, but some one to nurse me I *must* have, if there was one to be got, for it was plain I was not going to be up in a day. Mrs. Miller, our next neighbor, came in that evening—Frank went over and told her I was sick. She did a great many little things for me that made me feel a good deal better. I never was sensible before of how much value these *little things* are when we are weak and feeble, and how they brighten us up and seem to give us new life. Mrs. Miller consulted with Frank, and then came in and told me the plan they had been thinking of for my benefit. There was an Irish girl—Mary Donnelly—living at her brother's, a little out of the village, who wanted a place, and would be glad to come and do my work. She was a little raw, of course, having been but a short time over, but was a tidy, good-humored looking girl, and would no doubt do very well.

Then there was aunt Betsy Abby, an elderly woman, who had nothing in particular to do in the world except as she was picked up here and there by some one. She would gladly come and sit with me, and do little offices that I required; and she was really very kind and sympathizing, Mrs. Miller said, which she regarded as of much importance in a sick-room. She did not think I was going to be very sick; she had had those bilious attacks frequently since she had been in this climate, but they usually passed off in a little time without any thing very serious. They were generally brought on by overfatigue, as she thought mine was—for I had been house-cleaning—and with some mild medicine and quiet I would soon be better. It all seemed very reasonable, so I submitted to what Mrs. Miller and my husband proposed.

AUNT BETSY AND THE IRISH GIRL.

Aunt Betsy came. Frank showed her to the door of my room and disappeared. She may be an angel of comfort, I thought, but she *looks* like an *angle*—nay, more, like a *bundle of angles*. She was tall and bony—so bony that it seemed as if the skin merely was drawn over her *osseous* structure; and this same cuticle was decidedly saffron-like in hue. Her eyes—gooseberry eyes—had a sort of staring look, as if she never winked. Her hair was combed back behind her ears, and done up so tight and smooth that it looked like a coat of brown paint put on over the skin. A little nondescript-shaped cap, whose bright pink ribbons were sadly out of keeping with the sallow, shriveled face they were intended to adorn, was stuck on the back part of her head. It was a present, she informed me—from some one who had not a proper sense of the *fitness of things*—and was worn on the present occasion, I suppose, in honor of the minister's wife. The boundary line of her waist divided her into two equal parts, so far as I could judge without actual measurement, though if there was any difference the longitude was in favor of the upper portion. She had on a cheap delaine, sprinkled with bright red flowers, and a blue check apron of ample dimensions, which was worn in consideration of her *nursely duties*. She came up to my bedside—she did not stand till I had made this inventory of her charms.

"How do you do?" she asked grimly; and I noticed that her voice had a nasal twang.

I told her I hoped to be better soon, and she

sat down in a chair by the side of the bed and stared straight into my face. At last, as the result of her observation, she ejaculated, "Ye look desp'ret maugre!" I don't think the good woman understood a word of French, though the term she used sounded like it. "Yer man said I'd better see ef ye'd have somethin' t' eat. What'll ye have?" She seemed to shoot these words at me like a succession of bullets. Her presence oppressed me, so I told her I would have some toast and tea. She disappeared at once, and I drew a sigh of relief.

In a very short space of time she returned with a tray, upon which a clean napkin was spread, and a small plate of toast and a cup of tea were smoking. The toast was a nice brown and fixed just right, and the tea tasted fresh and good. I had not really felt any appetite when I told her I would have some supper, but I ate the greater portion of what she brought me. It was so nice that it created an appetite. "After all," I said to myself, "my nurse is better than she looks." She had another desirable quality for the sick-room; her tread was *velvety* as that of a cat. "We shall get along very well together," I thought. "I shall become accustomed to her grim looks. She is neat, quiet, and expeditious, and knows how to prepare a nice morsel, and we can not expect every thing." She seemed to know what I wanted without telling; she placed the pillows just right, for I was restless and feverish that evening, and wished them changed often, and I congratulated myself that I had a gem of a nurse, though in an uninviting setting.

The Irish girl came up the next day to fetch something that was wanted. She was a fresh, good-humored looking lass, presenting as strong a contrast to the individual who presided over *my* destinies as could well be imagined. I fancied I really felt revived and strengthened by the sunshine she brought with her, and I fear some rebellious thoughts with regard to the reigning power found their way into my mind;

such as, "I could bear with a few Irish *blunders* to have her about me. She seems to bring a wholesome air with her. What is the nice performance of a few mechanical arrangements to an influence of this kind that I feel so sensibly?" and I glanced involuntarily at my ogre-looking guardian, and could not help contrasting her with the fresh-looking Irish maiden. Whether my Medusa was intuitive, and divined something of what was passing in my mind to her disadvantage, or whether it was owing to a natural antagonism between the parties, I know not, but from that hour hostilities began between the two parties.

THE PROGRESS OF HOSTILITIES.

Aunt Betsy, as if to do away with any false preference I might have conceived for her rival, and also, I suppose, to give vent to a measure of dislike she could not contain, scarcely ever came to my room without detailing to me some impudence on the part of Mary toward herself, or some act of wastefulness or lack of neatness that she thought would rouse my indignation on my own account. I deducted a good deal from these relations on the score of antipathy, for I saw that aunt Betsy's was as inveterate toward her Irish companion as was that of Miss Ophelia to her colored *protegé,* and she had not the same principle and resolution to endeavor to overcome it. She would come to me with the information that Mary had upset the swill pail, and therefore the pig was defrauded of his supper; that she had left the tea-kettle on the hot stove without any water in it; or, what annoyed me most, she did not cook a mouthful for my husband to eat fit to set before a pig; and of course this was aside from her own duties, and she seemed to take a special delight in making a parade of Mary's shortcomings in this particular. Bringing me up a piece of toast nicely browned, she would say, "This don't look much like the toast of *that Irish girl*"—spoken with contemptuous emphasis, as though it was the most degrading of epithets—"it do n't look much like the toast she made for yer man's supper"—she always called Francis *my man*—"burnt as black as my shoe. O, sech an oncivilized pack as *these Irish* are! I wish to massy there was a law ag'in' any more on 'em comin' over. They're so dirty, no body can live in the house with 'em."

As she stood there giving vent to her indignation I saw a shadow flit past the door. Had Mary been listening? My suspicions with regard to this matter were soon confirmed, for when aunt Betsy went down to prepare my supper up came Mary, and after inquiring, "How do ye find yerself now, mum?" she spoke what was in her mind.

"Plase, mum," she said, "the old 'oman says I'm a dirty spalpeen, mum; but I'm not to the half so dirty as the likes o' her, that takes snuff right over yer porridge, mum, as I seen her doin' that same jist now, mum."

I recoiled with a sickening feeling from the image presented to my mind.

"Are you *sure*, Mary?" I asked. "I thought aunt Betsy was very neat."

"Indade, it's meself that *is* sure, mum; an' she's feedin' her nose with that nasty stuff the whole blessed time, mum, when yer eye's not on her, mum."

Here was a revelation that *struck home!* It was absolutely certain that I could not swallow another mouthful of aunt Betsy's preparing, however inviting it might *look*. When she came up with my gruel I declined tasting it, on the plea that I felt sick at my stomach, which was really true. Aunt Betsy was greatly concerned thereat, and tried to induce me to taste a little; she thought it would "settle my stomach." I could not; but still I felt faint, and as though I needed some nourishment, and I was at a loss what to do. Matters had come to a crisis.

THE DENOUEMENT.

In my extremity I resolved to send for Mrs. Harrington, and see if she could extricate me from the dilemma in which I was placed; for I felt too weak and spiritless to devise any means to effect this for myself. She had been absent on a journey for some weeks, and had arrived home only the night before, so she had not visited me since my illness.

She soon came in with her frank, good-humored, energetic-looking face, and I felt as if my case would be safe in her hands. She laughed when I told her who my nurse was, and my perplexity with regard to her. "Taking snuff," she said, "is not aunt Betsy's greatest failing. She eats opium." Now, I had a great repugnance to opium-eaters. The thought of having one about me in my then weak state filled me with horror. What was to be done? Aunt Betsy had really been very kind to me in her way, and had shown every assiduity to make me as comfortable as lay in her power, and I did not like to hurt her feelings; still, *something* must be done, for it was clear I could not live without nourishment, and it was just as certain that I could not take any more from her hands.

Mrs. Harrington, with her accustomed promptness, disposed of the matter in a summary manner. "Tell her," she said, "that she and the Irish girl do not agree—that *she*, of course, can not do the work below stairs, and that, therefore, you will be obliged to try and get along with Mary. I'll arrange it," she said, rising quickly; and before I had time to object, if I had wished, she had left the room, and I heard her tripping down stairs to fulfill her mission. The result was that aunt Betsy soon came up, looking any thing but dissatisfied with the turn affairs had taken, and, after expressing, in her way, her regrets at the necessity of leaving me, she went to her room, took her budget, and soon disappeared. So all parties were relieved by a little promptness of action on the part of my good friend, Mrs. Harrington.

"Now, I'll fix you some supper," she said; and she ran down stairs, and soon came up with a bowl of gruel, of which I partook heartily. After this, three times a day, for several days, she either sent me something from home, or came in and prepared it for me. She also gave instructions to Mary about performing her work in a proper manner. The girl was naturally intelligent, though *green* as her " own native isle of the ocean," and she improved so much under the tuition of Mrs. Harrington that she was soon able to prepare a dish of gruel equal to aunt Betsy herself, and which I could partake of without fear of *foreign seasoning*. She could also boil my husband's eggs, broil his steak, and make his coffee in the most approved manner.

CHAPTER X.

TALKS, ACTS, AND REFLECTIONS.

FATHER BRADEN AND MISS LESLIE'S COOK BOOK.

Father Braden came in to-day, and I ever find his conversation instructive. When he came in, I sat examining Miss Leslie's Receipt Book, to see if I could find some new dish to concoct for supper out of the materials at my command. He is very watchful over my moral and mental improvement, and seeing me lay the book upon the mantle-shelf when he came in, he inquired what I had been reading. I told him a little hesitatingly—I do n't know why.

"Ah, that is right—that is right!" said he, in his emphatic manner. "It is said that better lessons of the heart may be learned from a book of that sort than from the Sorrows of Werter; and I believe it."

"Yes," I answered, "if it be also true, as has been alleged, that 'the shortest way to a man's heart is through his stomach.'"

"The state of the heart, and of the head too, for that matter, depends a good deal on that of the stomach—that's pretty certain; therefore a good cook is a public benefactor," he replied; and he said one case was recorded where a man's heart had been reached directly through his stomach. It was that of Cooke, the actor, who married a cook of beefsteaks because she prepared one exactly to his mind. "But I'm glad to see that you desire to excel in household duties. A woman who presides well over a household, and keeps all its machinery in order, moral as well as material, performs an important part in life. To do this, calls for the exercise of qualities of the highest order. A woman who does this is a genius, and is more worthy to bear trophies, and have her brow wreathed with laurels, than the general who is successful on the battle-field, or one who writes words of burning eloquence. The most homely detail of this matter, if it has a use—if it furthers human happiness and improvement, has a beauty and a glory. Yet how many think these things, even the supervision of them, beneath them!"

I said I thought there was danger of a woman's confining her thoughts too closely to the trivial details of housekeeping—danger for those who took upon them household duties at all, and getting into a habit of being constantly "careful and troubled about many things" till her mind became petty and narrowed. I had known many women, of fine natural qualities, I told him, who *might*, if they had guarded against this belittling influence, not only have been good housekeepers, but something more, whose minds had become gradually narrowed, and the range of their ideas circumscribed, till they lost their relish for conversation or pursuits unconnected with their daily routine.

That result should be guarded against," he said, " and a woman should try to keep her mind open and active by proper reading and improving society, if she would be a *whole* woman. She must not let any of her faculties become dull from disuse. She should know, not only how to minister to the physical comfort of others, but her sympathies should be cultivated, that she may soothe in sorrow—her understanding enlightened, that she may counsel and guide—and her taste and imagination refined, that she may beautify and adorn life; and this not by the usual *outward accomplishments*, as they are termed, which, I think, considering the time, labor, and expense they cost, did not bring an equivalent in the pleasure their exercise gave to their possessor, or enabled her to confer upon others."

How much more noble, he said, the *art of conversing well!* And those who had talents that would enable them to excel in this most desirable art should endeavor to cultivate them with this view; and those who were not endowed with an aptitude in this respect could fill up the gaps by the display of their *accomplishments*. Those who aimed to do good in the world—to win hearts to them—desired to instruct or amuse, should endeavor to be good conversationalists in the true sense of that term, which was no slight thing.

LENDING BOOKS.

People often show niggardliness in the matter of books, when they would not display it in any other way—when they will expend great amounts to entertain others at their houses—make feasts for them—will bestow bread and clothing upon the hungry and naked! But do they sufficiently consider the needs of the intellectually famishing—the intellectually bare—those who need books to supply social lacks—who, with social longings, are, by circumstances perhaps, cut off from society? A few dollars expended in books to be lent to those who have intellectual tastes, but lack the means of gratifying them is often one of the best methods of dispensing charity, not only so far as conferring present pleasure is concerned, but lasting and substantial benefit—benefit to the mind from the nutriment afforded to it, for an active intellect requires food to sustain it as well as the body—benefit in the teaching good books may convey, in the amusement and relaxation they may afford to the overtasked in body, heart, or brain. This will be relief from the monotony of a dull life—an unvarying round of duties to which some are chained by circumstances, often tasks that are distasteful, and these weary most. How we can lighten the burdens of such with a little book, refreshing their overwearied faculties! And it is not like alms to the body, because what nourishes and refreshes one may be made to nourish and refresh many more. The history of one little book that has done duty in this way for years could tell a better tale of hearts lightened, irritable tempers soothed, heavy tasks made light, than that of many thousands of dollars ostentatiously bestowed.

GOOD ADVICE IN RHYME.

Jane Allen came in this evening. Seeing me writing, "Write something for me—some verses; give me some good advice—something I can keep to ruminate on," she said, in her flippant way, trying to look serious; but the roguish dimples *would* break around the corners of her mouth— the mischief *would* peep out of her eyes.

"Well, what shall I write?" I asked, suspending my pen above the paper. "Which of your faults shall I scourge?"

"O, I do n't know; there 's so many of them!" she answered. "Aunt Alice said to-day that I was eaten up by vanity; that I thought of nothing but dress—chasing the fashions and attracting the beaux. She said I would much sooner tear up a book for curl-papers than read it; and she told about a Scotch girl who tore up a book a minister had given her to read in this way; and when he saw her he said, 'You 've put the ornaments on the wrong side o' yer head, lassie.'

Perhaps you'd better write something about that. I'll show it to aunty; may be she'll have hopes of me," she said demurely.

I took the pen and wrote a few lines—doggerel, I suppose; but I will put them down here. Perhaps I may better them some day:

> On dress your best thoughts fritter not away—
> On outward ornament, show, and display.
> Your time and pains much better given, you'll find,
> Bestowed to dress and ornament your mind.
> Modes change not here, but what will charm to-day
> Will still enchant until life's latest ray.
> Good sense and wit, with manners void of art,
> Sweet tones and smiles fresh springing from the heart
> Will always bring you admiration true:
> Seek, then, these charms, substantial, ever new.

ECONOMY IN LITTLES.

I think if there is any class of people who should understand economy—economy in little things, the art of making a little go a great way—it is the class to which we belong. And a great deal can be learned in this matter. Much is lost often in every department of a household from want of care, want of thought, based mainly upon a want of knowledge. I know it was so with me in the beginning—I have learned much—I know there is need that I should learn much more. I must see why it is that some families dress respectably and live comfortably upon the same income that others receive who are always behindhand, look shabby, and have a poor table—have literally nothing to eat, and nothing to wear, and lay up nothing besides. With regard to clothes, I know there is much in repairing—in the art of making "auld claithes look maist as well as new." Some neglect to exercise this art from indolence—many from want of proper reflection. They do not see how much may be saved in this way with a very little trouble—without any detriment to appearances.

I thought to-day how much of all the labor in the world is vain, or the fruits of it wasted! A little in this household, a little in that, how much it amounts to in the aggregate! How much of the food that it costs such labor and expense to produce is wasted in this way, bringing no good to any one! How much of the material for clothing is absolutely thrown away, or used when it is not needed! Schools should be established to teach the importance of economy in little things; for it is from want of thought, want of knowledge, want of reflection in this matter that most women fail. They only see their little wastes, and do not consider how much these in every household diminish the general stock.

But it is not for reasons of public good alone, nor first that I would have women realize the importance of these things. Their duty to their families should be primarily considered; and if each woman does her duty to her family strictly, truly, she does her duty to the State, not only in matters of economy, saving so as not to diminish the general stock, but, if she be a mother, in the quality of those she rears and sends out to the help and support of the public good, as well as to found other homes from which the same good influence may go forth.

Woman, do you know how much of the prosperity, the happiness of the country depends upon you — your individual efforts? If every mother, every head of a household, did strictly her duty, from an enlightened and elevated point of view, how would the land be blessed by it, and how would individual happiness be increased!

LIVE IN A CHEERFUL ROOM.

We have four neighbors in sight, or at least four neighbors' houses. They might as well be prisons, for the most part, for any signs of cheerfulness or human habitation we see about them, except when there is company—shutters closed, like prison-bars, across the entire front of these houses, all these bright Summer days. Three of them have nice yards in front, filled with shrubs and flowers for other people's eyes, it must be, for their owners never seem to take any delight in them except to keep them in order. These owners are hired gardeners; their pay is—the applause of others.

The houses all have nice, pleasant front rooms, but their inhabitants eat, sleep, and sit in narrow, close, ill-lighted, and ill-ventilated back ones, keeping the front sedulously closed lest a ray of light, a breath of air, a fly, or speck of dust should intrude.

How can people bear to live so, cutting themselves off from what might be a pleasure and a delight every day of their lives? How health and cheerfulness would be promoted by living in light, airy, bright-looking rooms! People's spirits, and their tempers even, are affected by the aspect of things around them when they are not aware of it. How often they feel peevish and dissatisfied, heavy and complaining, when the remedy for these states lies right at their hand, and they know it not!

Whatever makes us cheerful promotes our health, and health promotes cheerfulness. Who does not know this? Yet we act as though we knew it not. If we can not afford to have the light and air come into our rooms because there is something in them that these will spoil, then throw these things out of the window, and rejoice in the air and sunlight. A plainly-furnished room to which these heavenly messengers have access, looks far more beautiful to me than one with splendid furniture with this prison gloom upon it. And then health is actually promoted by the air and sunlight, besides the favorable reaction produced upon it by our mental state when the breeze and the sunshine make us cheerful.

MOFFAT, THE CRUEL BUTCHER.

I made a decision to-day which I think, on reflection, was right, or rather I reconsidered a former decision. Moffat, the butcher from whom we have usually got our Winter supply of meat, was guilty of wanton cruelty to an animal he was about to slaughter. I do n't like to write it here, it so shocked me when I heard of it. I said then, and felt, I can never eat another mouthful of meat that passes through his hands. "The whole community," I said, "ought to refuse to patronize him; it was a duty." Frank abhors cruelty to animals as much as I do, and when I spoke to him about it he said, "Yes, we will go to some one else." And so we have done now for some time.

Meeting Moffat the other day, I saw he had a guilty, down look. He avoided my eyes at first, but when he looked at me there was an appealing look in his eyes that awoke my pity. It seemed to say—for he knew why we had neglected him; I had taken care, in my pharisaical spirit, that he should do so—his look seemed to say, "Do not condemn me for the indulgence of a propensity that was unchecked in early life. I have not been taught self-control like you; my unbridled passions carried me away with them."

After I went home I sat down and thought, "Is not this man entitled to pity that he has a proneness to anger he can not control? Is it not his misfortune that he was early subjected to influences that waked up angry passions instead of teaching him to subdue them? Are not, in this case, the sins of the parents visited upon the children?"—for I had heard that his parents were always involved in domestic broils, besides being contentious among their neighbors. "Anger is a short-lived madness," and he was insane from anger at the moment he treated the ox so cruelly. He is sorry, I can see. Harsh treatment is not going to mollify a nature like that; it will only harden him more. Perhaps he is not unsusceptible to softening influences. Coming in contact with natures different from his own will operate upon him insensibly. He may be benefited, and no one will be harmed.

I was going to write something more last night, but was interrupted. I was going to say, How often this spirit—"I am more holy than thou"—prevents our benefiting those who have wandered from the path of right! Suppose a missionary sent to heathen lands should intrench himself in his own righteousness, and refuse to come in contact with the benighted souls around him, how would his mission be fulfilled? Have we not heathens here? May not a timely word or one silent influence benefit them? Should we hold ourselves aloof from such for fear of pollution? Did we possess sufficient of the spirit of Christ, we could impart to them without receiving injury, and we should delight to do so.

CHAPTER XI.

SURPRISES AND BLESSINGS.

A VISIT FROM MY PARENTS.

O, JOY! I did not think there was such happiness on earth for me. But I must compose my thoughts, and record this joyous incident of my life in sober language. Frank had gone to spend the evening with brother Mason, who is seriously ill, and had particularly requested it, leaving me alone. I felt unusually lonely—a sort of heavy feeling, as though I would lay my head in my mother's lap as when a child.

I suffered my thoughts to dwell upon my early home, the affection that had been lavished upon me there, and the happiness I had enjoyed, more than I have done, I believe, at any time since my marriage. A sort of vague feeling of regret took possession of me. Tears welled up and filled my eyes; they overflowed, and I indulged in a good fit of crying, the first for a long time; for Frank does not like to see me in tears, and I think we can control ourselves in this respect in a great measure. I heard the gate open and shut, and then steps coming up the walk, and voices. "It is some of the neighbors," I thought, "and I must wipe my eyes and go to the door. What will they think to see the minister's wife in tears? I fear they will think she is dissatisfied with them, or her husband, when the truth is she is most dissatisfied with herself." I wiped my eyes hastily, and went to the door.

When I opened it I thought two unrealities stood there. Involuntarily I clasped my hands before my eyes to shut out what seemed a vision. They were torn away; a pair of arms of unmistakable muscle were thrown around me, clasping me so closely I could scarcely breathe, while kisses were rained upon my cheeks and lips. It was my mother. When she released me my father—for he was with her—raised me in his strong arms, as he used to do when I was a child, and carried me back to the sitting-room, the door of which I had left open, and sat down with me on his lap.

"You have been crying," said my mother, when the lamp shone on my face, discovering with the quick eye of maternal tenderness the traces of tears upon it.

"It is nothing," I answered, a little confusedly. "I was sitting here alone, and I got to thinking of old times, and I cried a little. You know I used to cry often, but I have not lately; I don't know when before."

I had an instinctive fear that they would think my married life unhappy, finding me alone and in tears, and I explained to them that Frank was unavoidably absent, on a visit to a sick brother. I talked of—I don't know what—a little of every thing—all at once, I guess, and asked—I don't know how many questions; and I had to shed a few more tears, too, for joy and surprise this time—my mother taking off her own things and laying them on the table, for I was so excited and bewildered I did not think to do it for her.

"But you haven't had supper," I exclaimed, bethinking myself suddenly, and jumping up from my father's lap.

"No," said my mother; "your father wanted to get it at the tavern—as it was so late, he thought you would be through supper—but I told him I thought it would be so much pleasanter to take it with you."

"O, it will be such a pleasure," I exclaimed, "to prepare a meal for you, and sit down and eat it with you once more!" And the tears sprang to my eyes again, but I dashed them away, and, lighting a candle, I said, "I will go to the kitchen and get you something to eat, and then you will have more strength to answer my questions, and talk as fast as I want to have you."

"O, give us any thing you've got! Don't

A VISIT FROM MY PARENTS. 199

go to cooking any thing," said my mother; and father said, "Yes." But I told them I chose to get something warm, and have the table set cozily, and sit down and eat with them, for I had not had half a supper myself, Frank being away. The stove was not cold, and I could make them some hot tea in a few minutes, and I liked to have my own way as well as ever, I laughingly said to my father. My mother insisted that she would help me, and so she went with me to the kitchen. Father said he could get along alone very well for a while; and he supposed we would want to talk over some privacy—women always did.

The fire was soon roaring, and the tea-kettle singing; and O! how happy I was, talking with my mother and bustling about, trying to do something, but always forgetting what I was after—making my mother laugh by bringing the mustard instead of the soda to put in the griddle-cakes that I thought I would make especially for my father, for he is very fond of them.

What a revulsion of feeling! I thought I had never been so wretched since my marriage as I was one hour before; I had never been so happy as I was now. I did not ask my mother how it had all happened that they came. They were there, and that was enough for the present. I did not like to question my happiness, for fear it would fly away. I saw my mother look at me anxiously once in a while. I knew the marks of tears in my face troubled her; but I was not going to say any thing to convince her that I had found all the happiness I expected in my married life, and more. I knew this would be evident to her if she remained with me a few days, and I did not want to admit the possibility of its being questioned; though I knew as well as if she had spoken it that she had some fears on this point that caused her troubled glances at me.

My father and mother staid with me three days—three happy days they were to me. My father's business would not permit him to remain longer, though I pleaded earnestly with him to do so. But he promised to come again soon, and perhaps leave my mother to spend a few weeks with me. My mother told me before they went away, how it happened that they came. I felt very anxious to know all the time, but somehow did n't like to ask. He came in, the evening before they set off, and surprised her by saying:

"I have some business near M., and must start to-morrow. Suppose you go along, and we will go out of our way a little, and see Laura."

I had been his idol, and probably his heart had been relenting toward me for a long time, though he had not spoken of it.

A SMALL HOUSE NOT AN EVIL "PER SE."

We have a small house here, yet it is sufficient for our needs on ordinary occasions. Extraordinary ones rarely occur; and "better a house too small one day than too large all the year." Who was it that replied, when told by some one that there was not room in his house to swing a cat, "Sir, I do not want to swing a cat." It is very good philosophy to endeavor to conform our desires to our circumstances. This is my theory. I do not always employ it in practice, I fear. An old lady said consolingly to me to-day, "You will have the less to clean." My thoughts went prospecting forward to the event of a donation-party, as I surveyed the narrow rooms; but I thought it could be managed by throwing open the chambers. At any rate, I will borrow no trouble for the future.

SARAH GRIFFITH.

I have had a letter from Sarah; and O, such a patient, resigned spirit breathes through it! Ah! I can never attain her saintliness of temper. I am too much of "the earth, earthy." How much she must suffer!—not only physical pain, but those pangs of the spirit, harder to be borne. Hope deferred—tnat sickness of the heart—and a lack of sympathy, so wounding to the sensitive soul. But she hopes and trusts through all that brighter days will come; and I feel a conviction that her sweet resignation and unswerving faith will meet a reward here.

TARNISHED BY THE RUST OF GAIN.

I have been reading to-day an old book of proverbs of all nations. How much wisdom is done up in these little bundles! Some of them—many of them are fallacious, and, no doubt, mislead. The proverbs of Poor Richard, it is said, have done much mischief, in making us a nation of money-getters; but then the proverbs were well enough, only we carried them too far. And what a great evil it is that the desire of wealth should be allowed to swallow up every other consideration, as it does almost with many, and be made the chief object of life!

How dwarfing to all the noble faculties of the soul this exclusive pursuit of riches! Justice, benevolence—all the higher and finer qualities of the man are often laid upon the altar of this blind desire of gain. As in the fable of the nymph who was changed to a tree, this "creeping rind" of avarice encroaches and encroaches till the whole nature is incased with it. Grasp, grasp—nothing else for a lifetime! How debasing! And the nice sense of justice and of right becomes blunted in this grasping process, while the grasper fancies that might means right, and with a thousand sophistries bolsters the belief that what, weighed by the nice scales of justice, would be the property of another, is his own; for,

"When self the wavering balance shakes,
It's rarely right adjusted."

I am glad I did not marry a man who was in danger of becoming incrusted — of having his finer nature tarnished, by this moth and rust of gain. Truly, a minister of the Gospel, so removed from the temptations that beset men in ordinary life, ought far to excel them in all the virtues! Do they improve as they should the advantages of their condition?

MOODS IN WRITING OR CONVERSATION.

Certain conditions are necessary to success in writing—certain mental and physical conditions; though what would be favorable to one would not be to another, differently constituted. The state of things around us influences the flow of our ideas, and the grace and facility with which we clothe them. It seems to me that almost every writer has some pet whim which it is necessary to indulge in order to write his best. I—I do n't mean to class myself among known writers, but I *write*, and can write better under some circumstances than others—I was going to say that my ideas flow more freely, and their proper clothing comes to me more readily when all is pleasant and harmonious around me, and I myself feel in calm and placid mood, and am perfectly at ease physically. I can write better directly after a generous meal than fasting. To be sure, this would not be the case if I should eat to heaviness; but when I have eaten just what my system requires to strengthen and refresh me, and of the kind of food that suits it best.

It seems to me that, instead of the style of a writer being always the same, it must vary to suit different moods of mind, or as exciting causes change.

Sometimes I can dash off something nervous and pointed after some sudden mental excitement, but do not reason so calmly and clearly as in a more equable state of mind.

In conversation we do not always feel disposed to talk in the same strain. Sometimes we are inclined to be witty and lively; again, grave and reflective, or to trifle easily, perhaps, and clothe nothings with interest; and so we change our style of talking to suit our differing phases of thought, feeling, and emotion. And people who differ from themselves thus are the most pleasing companions. They do not tire by their sameness. Now, the best written and most instructive book wearies, if written throughout in the same strain. Sparkle upon sparkle of wit, or a dead level of sentiment, or moralizing, or any form of sameness, tires. To be sure, in the talker and writer there is a certain individuality preserved through all their variations.

. . . .

I had to leave off, and I hardly know what I have been saying, or what I began about in the first place. Perhaps it is just as well—only I like to put down my resolutions for improvement, and my progress in it. It seems to assist and strengthen me to give a form to my resolves, and to record my success or failures in regard to keeping them, so that I can look back occasionally, and see what ground I have gained. In no other way, I am afraid, could I perceive that I have advanced; and I might become discouraged in view of the trifling attainments I make in the directions I have proposed to myself. On the other hand, I wish to keep my shortcomings in view, to avoid too great fallings-off in regard to the pursuit of these various improvements. To these ends I have a plan, and each night jot down how near I come up to it. I find this admirable for preventing the time from slipping away unimproved; besides, I find a real enjoyment in it.

IMPORTANCE OF TRIFLES.

Father Braden was in to-day, and we had a discourse upon the importance of trifles, and some of the thoughts that were brought out I wish to fix in my memory for future use and reference.

"Nothing is a trifle that has power to affect human happiness." A moment seems a trifle, but on the act, the decision of a moment, may hang our destiny for time and eternity. We are prone to forget that an aggregation of littles makes an important whole. It is so with savings; it is so with time; it is thus with our endeavors, our little gainings in the way of excellence. One new thing learned every day, and what a mass of information will soon accumulate!

Words are little things, but they are sometimes keener than a two-edged sword—sharper than a serpent's tooth. Light in seeming, they sometimes fall on the heart with a crushing weight. A word carelessly spoken will separate friends. Where suspicion or jealousy exists, how carefully must our words be chosen; for

> "Trifles light as air
> Are to the jealous confirmation strong
> As proofs of Holy Writ."

Napoleon said, "There are no such things as trifles." There are not, if we look at results. The great fault of life is, that we do not prize the moments as they fly. They are "the stuff that life is made of—the golden sands of time." "Take care of the moments, and the hours will take care of themselves."

> "Still on it creeps,
> Each little moment at another's heels,
> Till hours, days, years, and ages are made up
> Of such small parts as these, and men look back,
> Worn and bewildered, wondering how it is!"

A few moments with a bad book, some one said, gave a moral taint to his nature, which time could not eradicate. A word dropped in the presence of a child may infuse a moral poison into his mind that may tend to destroy the healthfulness of his whole being.

> "We waste, not use, our lives; we breathe, not live.
> Time wasted, is existence; used, is life;
> And bare existence man, to live ordained,
> Wrings and oppresses with enormous weight."

A writer has said, "The pivot upon which our whole future destiny may hang is often so small as scarcely to be noticed." A word, a look, the lightest action of a person's life, may be fraught with consequences that will shake his soul to its center. Some philosopher said, "The stamp of a man's foot may move the universe."

A VISIT TO MY CHILDHOOD'S HOME.

I have been on a visit to my own early home, and have been very happy. Though I shed some natural tears at the revival of old memories, and at the sight of things once familiar, they were not tears of bitterness. No lingering regret that I had left these scenes and cast my lot in different places mingled with my emotions upon seeing them again.

I can hardly tell why I wept, for I am not one of those who "expand the lachrymal gland easily," as Henry expresses it. Indeed, I always feel rather ashamed of displaying feeling in this way, because I have seen so many women who have a habit of resorting to tears to elicit sympathy or gain petty ends, and in such cases it always looks to me weak and unwomanly, or implying dissimulation. So I always try to keep back mine; but now a kind of tender, sad feeling came over me, and tears welled over before I was aware they were coming. Frank looked troubled when he saw them—they are so unusual. I laughed when I saw the serious shade that came over his face, and speedily my tears were dried, proving merely an "*April shower*," as he was pleased to observe.

Placing myself in former circumstances, showed me how much I have changed, and, comparing myself with former associates, I feel that I have improved somewhat. One evening, finding in a closet an old dress I used to wear, I put it on, and, arranging my hair in former fashion, came to the supper-table. They all laughed at my metamorphosis, and said it was the Laura of old. I did not tell them that I did not feel at all like the wrong-headed girl I once was. Not that I am more unhappy; I feel far happier—a deeper, fuller content, a more realizing sense of the blessings that attend me, of the many pleasant circumstances that are around my path, and of the various opportunities for improvement that I enjoy, and which I hope I do not wholly waste. So I felt like enjoying every thing and regretting nothing.

READING BOOKS AND OBSERVING MEN.

We can all, without neglecting any of the immediate duties of life find time to improve our minds by proper reading, and, so far from sustaining any loss by so disposing of a portion of our time, we find great gain, even in a pecuniary point of view. We must understand our duties in the various relations of life in order to ,be successful, or to secure our happiness.

What gain there is in knowing *the best way of doing things*, not only if we have a piece of work to do, but in all our conduct! How much of the misery of life comes from "*doing things wrong*," not voluntarily, knowingly, but blindly, ignorantly! And we have not always sufficient wisdom in ourselves to guide us aright; nor do those with whom we are associated, who assume to teach us, always possess it. In books, well selected, we can converse with the wisest and best, and receive the benefit of their wisdom and experience.

Yet we should not neglect, at the same time, to learn from persons about us, not only by precept, but from their example, to follow or shun. See how wrong-doing looks in others—note its consequences—then apply the test to ourselves, and remove the beam from our own eyes. Remember that what looks bad to us in others, looks as much so in us to them; and if their ill-conduct bring unhappy results to them, it will do so equally in our own case.

NATURALNESS AND AFFECTATION.

"The fool hath planted in his mind an army of good words," said father Braden, when we returned this evening from a lecture given by a young man—a stranger, Mr. Stanley—wherein he endeavored to edify us upon the subject of "Æsthetics," which reminded me of the Scotchman's definition of metaphysics—"What nae body kens, and what the mon does na ken himsel'."

I fear he found an unappreciative audience; that is, so far as the subject and object of his lecture were concerned. There were some whose sense of the ridiculous enabled them to appreciate the *absurdity* of the affair. While he stood there before us, pouring from behind his well-trimmed mustache a perfect torrent of fine words and phrases, to which the ideas and meaning they conveyed bore about as great a proportion as a kernel of wheat to a bushel of chaff, I thought he proved himself a true logician in the art he showed, of "talking unintelligibly about what he did not understand." And he mouthed and ranted like a school-boy uttering his declamation, seeming to imagine, as many speakers do, that by this means he would render what he said more effective, when, if they only knew how much more impressive a simple natural manner is, not tame, but animated by an earnestness, and prompted by a true interest in the subject, they would spare themselves much unnecessary muscular exertion, and run less danger of bronchitis, from speaking in a strained, unnatural tone.

I have no doubt he thought he was astonishing his simple, unlearned audience by a brilliant rhetorical and philological display, in which his white ringed fingers bore a conspicuous part. Indeed, his gestures reminded one of brushing away imaginary musketoes.

How much trouble people give themselves in various ways to depart from Nature, when following her would render them much more efficient and pleasing! Nature may be improved, but must not be outraged. It is so in manners. Many endeavor to attain perfection in this respect by a laborious affectation, when, by being simple and natural, they would appear much better. It is so in writing—composition—too palpable endeavors after a fine style often spoil what would otherwise be a tolerable book. It is thus in matters of dress. True beauty and harmony are often destroyed by elaborateness in this particular.

In public speaking, most of all, I have been distressed to see what unnatural tones and gestures sometimes mar a fine discourse. We are so prone to overdo in externals where approbation is sought; yet the fault often arises from a desire after perfection, and a want of confidence in our own powers. We are afraid to trust to their natural outflow.

DARKENED ROOMS AND HEALTH.

There is one thing I have outgrown the taste for, and that is darkened rooms. I hope it is because my knowledge has advanced, or my knowledge of human physiology, at least. "Our taste declines with our merit," it is said; so it ought to keep pace with it upward. People know that light is necessary to plants to make them grow and thrive well; they do not know, all of them, that it is just as essential to their own health and vigor. How many things there are to prove this! but people will not see. Those who live in dark alleys or cellars are always sallow and miserable, liable to disease. It is even more so with those who live on the shady side of a street, it is said, than with those where the sunlight strikes free and unobstructed.

Staying one day in a partially-darkened room

will not affect the vigor of the constitution, but habitually living in one will most assuredly lower the vitality. Yet, because these causes work gradually and imperceptibly, people will not believe they exist; yet they work as surely as if a small quantity of some subtile poison were taken daily into the system, by slow degrees sapping the springs of life. Since I see these things more clearly, I wonder I ever lived so long careless and blind to them. How ignorant we are content to be, and how sinful and miserable in consequence! We shut out not only the light of heaven from our parlors, but the light of knowledge from our minds.

What if our carpets do fade, are they of more worth than the lives, health, and happiness of human beings? We do not like dimly-lighted rooms in the evening—they look gloomy to us. It is only a perverted taste that prevents darkened rooms looking less so in the daytime. Is sunlight less glorious than gaslight? But it reveals the defects in a lady's beauty—her complexion exposes her making up. Ah, did she live nearer to truth and nature, she would have fewer defects to be revealed—would not need cosmetics for her complexion, nor be obliged to resort to the shams of "making up!"

CHAPTER XII.

BOARDING AT MRS. PARKINSON'S.

A NEW STATE OF AFFAIRS.

A VERY unexpected turn of affairs: we are going to board at the widow Parkinson's. Frank came in this evening, and said that Mr. Nims, the proprietor of the house we have occupied since we have been in P., had returned from the West, and wanted to remove his house, to make some other use of it, if we had no objections to leaving it. Frank said he was rather glad of the opportunity, for he thought it would be better for us to board for a while. I must confess I was a little dismayed at the prospect at first; but on reflecting on the opportunities for mental improvement, which a greater degree of leisure would afford me, and the time I should have to put my wardrobe in order, as well as to

A NEW STATE OF AFFAIRS. 221

add to my inner furnishing, I concluded it was a fortunate chance, and that I might, if properly employed, reap advantages from it which would compensate me for the loss of fireside joys for a season, for we can not fully enjoy these at the hearth of another. So Frank went and conferred with the widow Parkinson, and it is all arranged.

How things work together for our good sometimes, when we distrust, and would alter the course of events! It is going to be so about this boarding of ours, I believe. Mrs. Miller is going to board for six months at the same place, during her husband's absence. I hope to improve by this close intercourse with her, as well as to gain pleasure from it.

She realizes more nearly my ideal of a "perfect woman nobly planned" than any I ever met. She is one of my sort of beauties, too, though she would n't generally be thought handsome. I love to watch her varying expression now melting into tenderness, then flashing with spirit.

There is so much variety about her; "she is ever pleasing, ever new;" still there is not the least fickleness; there is always the same sterling principle at bottom, the same noble feeling, firm purpose, and contempt of littleness, and upon this solid basis the ornamental part of her character is set and polished. I feel an expansion of being whenever I come into her presence—the influence is her largeness of soul.

We can read, walk, and talk together, and how it will brighten and give zest to my life! How her society will strengthen me to keep my resolutions still to attain higher degrees of excellence! How many aids I shall receive from her good sense and wider knowledge of life! I am truly grateful that such a blessing has fallen in my way, for it is just what I need. I hope no jealousies may arise from my partiality for her. I do not intend to show it in any offensive way, if I can avoid it. I think there is a mutual sympathy between us—I felt it—and I am glad.

I do not like to look forward to the fact, that

at the end of one or two years I must leave her. "Sufficient for the day is the evil thereof."

SCHEMING TO LIVE GENTEELLY.

I have been very busy for a few days, and now we are comfortably settled at our boarding place. We have a pleasant room, a fine prospect from the window, and I hope I shall enjoy my life here very much. This will depend something upon the sunshine I brew inside, I suppose.

Our landlady is not just the kind of woman I admire and respect, but I will not let this circumstance detract from my happiness, if I can avoid it. Perhaps I may even derive benefit from the defects I see in her. She is a woman devoted to dress and show, with small means to support these gods of her idolatry; therefore she is driven to scheming to compass her ends, and she has acquired a hard, calculating look from exercising these faculties so much. I do n't think there is any need of my guarding against this fault. I do n't believe there is any danger of my running into it—that is, planning. A little more of this faculty, perhaps, a little greater facility in exercising it, might be of advantage to me. I have sometimes found petty savings—contrivances to make both ends meet—extremely irksome, and have indulged in some impatient, possibly unreasonable, thoughts and feelings with regard to being obliged to do so. Yet how necessary it is in our circumstances that we understand the art of making the most of every thing! There is no meanness, no selfishness about this. It is wise—it is politic. Great minds have not disdained attention to this matter; and in many cases it is a real saving of labor to prevent waste, as often the labor it takes to remedy some negligence would more than have sufficed to prevent it.

And here those good old proverbs of Mrs. Ackley's come in: "An ounce of prevention is better than a pound of cure;" and, with regard to a constant stream of small wastes, which are sometimes regarded as trivial, "a little leak will sink a great ship." But there is a great difference between Mrs. Ackley's wholesome economy—though it may sometimes seem to those differently educated to be a little overstrained—and Mrs. Parkinson's scheming, and the ends are different. Mrs. Ackley acts from conscientious scruples, a desire that nothing shall be lost, and she does not withhold her hand from bestowing upon those who need what her care has given her to impart. I fear self-indulgence, vanity, the desire of gratifying a love of display, is the motive power of the other. And she pursues her end in a way which Mrs. Ackley would not. She endeavors to screw in a bargain, to grind those that work for her. (Bed-time.)

"A too eager pursuit of small profits—small savings—may disturb the equanimity of a mind that ought to be easy and happy."

The more I see of my landlady, Mrs. Parkinson, the more I am convinced that she has suffered circumstances to warp and pervert qualities in her character, that might, with a little different direction, and some pruning, have conduced to its symmetry and beauty. I have seen decidedly good women made of far worse original material. What a pity the best can not be made of every thing! What a pity for her, how unfortunate for her children, that her mind should be engrossed principally by frivolities, when it might have been occupied by higher aims, and her own and their happiness much increased thereby!

But it is useless moralizing—useless lamenting. I suppose the very best method we can take to better the world is, to endeavor to improve one individual in it—that person in whom we are supposed to be most particularly interested. This work done to its fullest extent, or at least fairly begun, then we may, perhaps, have some title to go missionarying among our neighbors. Still we naturally have that *benevolent* feeling that we like to see our neighbors shorn of faults whatever may happen to our own.

THE BLESSED FORTUNE OF HAVING FRIENDS.

How fortunate I am to find so many friends from whom I can learn something that will be of use to me! I think we may learn something of every one, if we desire; but these friends seem adapted to my particular needs.

From father Braden I get a good many useful hints upon moral conduct; from Mrs. Miller, a knowledge of life and manners I did not possess; and from old Mrs. Ackley I glean many lessons upon domestic affairs that I hope I may turn to advantage when I am again mistress of my own home. Such an episode of leisure may never occur in my life again, and I must employ it in laying up store for my working days that are to come. I do n't think this season of respite from care will give me a distaste for active employment when it becomes necessary. I think I shall be better fitted for its proper performance than before, and shall engage in it with a more hearty diligence.

I would not ask to live always the life I now lead. I fear I might grow selfish and indolent. "Life's cares are comforts," when we do not have too great a burden of them. And in most cases, when they are too heavy, we make them so. And how much useless labor there is in the world, labor for which no one is better or happier, and which does not "leave us leisure to be good!"

Mrs. Parkinson cultivates flowers, and I revel among them every day. There are children here, too — human flowers — true children, some of them, not those unnatural beings young in years, but old in heart. There is nothing more pleasant than the beautiful truthfulness of children; nothing more sad than to see this die out from the gradual influence of those about them, or by direct reproof teaching them to

> "Check the stars and sallies of the soul,
> And break off all its commerce with the tongue,"

or impressing upon them the spirit of the French proverb, that "the true use of speech is to conceal thoughts, not to express them." Angels must weep to see this perverting process applied to a fair young soul.

My life here has been gladdened by a sprightly boy of twelve, that like a flower sprung up in my pathway, refreshing, beautifying—like a ray of sunlight, brightening, warming—harmonizing like a strain of soft melody, soothing my spirit like healing balm. How sad to think that his unsullied nature must be tarnished, its fine gold become dim, its unselfishness be alloyed, its quick sympathies dulled, and its beautiful truthfulness become warped by intercourse with the world!

SOCIAL AND SELF-CULTURE.

Henry will board here with us a part of the time, and I hope he will help me persuade Frank to take a little more time for social intercourse. Henry will do so, though his Latin languish a little. He says his mental nature requires it, and is expanded, strengthened, and refreshed by it. I wish I could make Frank believe this, for he looks so pale and worn buried among his books so much.

He does know that it is true in the abstract; but he is so afraid he shall not acquit himself with credit to himself and his profession, and do all his duty, that he keeps putting off the time to attend to self, forgetting that he owes a duty there. I am sure I should be very sorry to have him prove a bungler, or to fail in any point in his calling; but I do not want to have him sacrifice himself.

I am so happy when I can win him from his books for an evening, and the weary look goes away from his face, and his eye comes out from behind its cloud of thoughtfulness, and shines brightly as it used to do. Father Braden often helps me to draw him away from his books, when his plea is, "a little longer."

THE ART OF CONVERSATION.

How I pity those who wish to render themselves agreeable and do n't know how! The more

THE ART OF CONVERSATION. 231

they try, the further they seem to be from the mark. They are no doubt tiresome to themselves as they are tedious to others, and they are often such good, well-meaning people, that we must tolerate them, and regard for their feelings prompts us to endeavor to seem pleased with them. Now, this is no slight trial, occurring so often as it does, considering the number of estimable people in the world, who are in no wise qualified to render themselves entertaining. I have been pained to see people show by their manner their impatience and distaste of these very worthy persons, who, in their efforts to be agreeable, succeed in making themselves very wearisome.

Now, there is an old couple living neighbors to us, so very kind, so truthful and upright, and possessing so many sterling qualities, that one can not but value them for these, but so utterly deficient in the art of conversation, so entirely barren of any topics that have not been worn thrice threadbare, that it is really a pain to listen to them, or would be, except for the pleasure it affords to endeavor to seem pleased with what they say, to gratify them, or at least to avoid hurting their feelings. I do not know of a better exercise for patience and forbearance than endeavoring to carry on a conversation with such persons for a few hours. It seems to me that a very small portion of tact and reflection would enable people to see, in some degree, what would be agreeable or otherwise to others, and be guided accordingly; but there are few persons who do not make signal mistakes in this matter of adapting conversation to time, place, and people. The residuum of most conversations is nothing. And they have not even succeeded in being pleasant in passing, for it is possible to pass a space of time occasionally in an agreeable manner, talking upon nothing, or trifles that are next to nothing; much more pleasant, and full as profitable, as to spend it in abstract disquisitions that amount to nothing, and would not better any one could the point be settled.

Now, this art of conversing agreeably and

profitably is a subject that I think deserves much more attention than it receives. Would n't it be a better mental discipline than the study of languages—a mere repetition of words that clog the memory, and do not render us any more fluent in expressing ourselves in our own language; that furnish us with no ideas for conversation, or food for thought, or lessons from which we may draw instruction to regulate our lives, or to impart for the benefit of others? To me there is something melancholy in the sight of a person wasting so much of his existence as is necessary to acquire a knowledge of ten, fifteen, or perhaps twenty, or even fifty languages. It always seems to me he must be a little insane. Language is of no value except as a medium of thought; and who is there to whom, in one short life, so many vehicles of imparting or receiving knowledge will be necessary?

This learning the use of so many tools, and never applying them to delve for knowledge or true wisdom, has seemed to me like this: suppose in every country there was a mine of gold and precious jewels, but that in each one the mode of obtaining these was different, and must necessarily be so, requiring the machinery to be used to be different in each case. Now, suppose in a man's own country there was more of this hidden treasure than he could use in his lifetime, which he could easily obtain, and that, after making himself master of the means of attaining it, or perhaps only imperfectly effecting this, he should set himself to learn the use of the tools of all other countries for the same purpose, without applying any of them, or at least doing so in a very slight degree to their proper purpose; how would we look on such a man?

But I have strayed away from the subject of talking agreeably, which was the theme I began upon, wandering off like my imaginary miner, delving a little here and there, and not effecting much any where, perhaps. Conversation need not always be of weighty matters. The discussion of trifles is not only sometimes pleasant and appropriate, but may be even rendered profitable. It is useful in one sense, if it is agreeable and enlivening, if it be not indulged too often to the neglect of more serious matters that should claim a due share of our attention. To be able to converse well, gracefully, agreeably, profitably, to have the tact to perceive just when to speak and when to be silent, just what to speak, where to speak, and to whom, is one of the highest accomplishments, and one most readily available under all circumstances. It is one by which we may not only render ourselves agreeable and acceptable, but by which, if we are benevolent, we may benefit others, as well as please and divert them. Some persons talk what would sound very well if we read it from a book, but their manner spoils all the pleasure we should otherwise derive from their conversation; or perhaps their voices are unpleasant, or their pronunciation defective.

With many otherwise good conversationists, there is too great an appearance of effort, the machinery is too visible, and it affects you somewhat, as you might be by hearing the prompter's whisper at the theater, or by the friction of the wood and iron in some musical instrument, spoiling the effect of the melody. But some people can not do any thing gracefully and smoothly. No amount of theoretical knowledge or drilling would enable them to do it.

A person who is able to talk well, in the highest import of that phrase and in the varieties of meanings it embraces, is as rare as one who is polite in the highest and best acceptation of that term, and it requires as rare a combination of qualities to produce the one as the other, and in many respects these are similar. The acquirements of most persons in both these particulars, the art of conversation and true courtesy, scarcely extend much beyond the surface of these matters. It is a little here and there, but is not full, complete, symmetrical—sufficient for all the circumstances of life. We neglect the weightier matters of the laws that govern in these respects, and make offerings of "mint, and anise, and cummin."

WILLIAM MARCY, OR A WARNING INCIDENT.

I do not like to dwell upon sad subjects. It is not pleasant for me, and I doubt if it is profitable to do so—that is, to form a habit of mind to select what is somber from the circumstances around us, and keep it before the mental vision. But sometimes the sad realities of life will thrust themselves before us, and shut out from our view the beautiful pictures our fancy is so fond of weaving, and which are pleasanter to contemplate than every day's report of the wrong and misery about us.

To-day, a saddening view was forced upon me, but perhaps it is wholesome to look at it. I must go back a little to make it clear. Ten years since, I met in a neighboring State, a gentleman named Marcy, who was then about thirty-five years of age. He was a merchant, and doing a flourishing business. He was not married. Early in life I learned he had wooed and won a beautiful girl, but death had snatched her from him. This was, for him, the "heart's ordeal," which, it is said, all must pass sooner or later. He recovered from it and was happy again. I think I never saw a person who seemed to have greater enjoyment of life than he. If there were any regrets for what he had lost, they were deep down in his heart, and did not often trouble the surface. Why should he not be happy? Young—younger than his years—no one would have taken him to be over twenty-five, or twenty-eight at most—healthy, a perfect model of health and vigor; of person and manners so agreeable, that he was acceptable every-where, enjoying, and conferring enjoyment in social life; prosperous in his worldly affairs, rapidly accumulating wealth. Why should he not have gone on enjoying to the end of his days—reaping enjoyment from even the sense of existence in his perfectly healthy body; tasting higher pleasures by means of his clear and well-stored mind? Who so privileged as he?

Yesterday, visiting Mrs. Allen, she said, " Mrs.

Congden, our next neighbor, has just had a brother brought home to her, who seems in the last stage of consumption. His name is William Marcy. He is from the West. Perhaps you have heard of him?"

I started. "William Marcy! Is it possible! I knew him. What could have brought consumption to him? Health seemed to have set its seal upon him."

I went with Mrs. Allen to call upon him. I could see no traces, except in the high and noble forehead, of the William Marcy of ten years ago. There he lay, looking so weak and pitiful, propped up in an invalid's chair; his abundant hair thinned to baldness; great dark hollows in his cheeks where the roses of health had bloomed; his eyes, that had so sparkled with life and intelligence, hollow and dim; his full, rich voice, weak and querulous; his form, so clothed with strength, and grace, and beauty, a meager skeleton, now bowed and wasted.

"Why is this?" I thought, as I took his thin,

weak hand. Was it inevitable? Who gave such promise of health and long life as he, of a life of happiness? Is it true, as a writer says, that "we are all failures?" Needs it be so? The answer came to me in some words I read many years ago, that made an impression on my mind: "To all, life might be freedom, progress, success. To most it is bondage, failure, defeat."

Why is it so? It is because we do not know how to live. We do not even know the simple rules that pertain to bodily health, which lies at the foundation of happiness and success. The man before me, I learned from his sister, had failed for want of this knowledge; had undermined his health gradually, but as surely, as if he had taken every day, for years, a small quantity of poison, sapping its foundation. She had visited him five years before, and warned him, but he heeded her not. He employed the day in business, confining himself in a close counting-room. The nights, till a late hour, he gave to reading or some amusement, going to the houses of his friends or receiving them at his bachelor lodgings. Wine, late suppers, were freely indulged in, and he went feverish and excited to bed. Worse, he was in the habit, in Winter, of sleeping in a close, heated room, arranging it so that the fire was kept up all night. This was his idea of luxury with regard to this matter. Was it any wonder that his health failed?

I could not shut out a train of sad reflections, called up by the sight of this wreck of manhood, made sadder still when I thought of the happiness he had lost when his sister told me he was engaged in marriage a year since to a worthy and beautiful woman. Are not these things frequent, without exciting our special wonder? I looked round among my friends and acquaintances, and I saw how many were failing, how many had failed, from want of proper knowledge of the conditions of health. Is it not criminal, I thought, to be so blind and ignorant, when the means of knowledge are so easy, so cheap? Men will barter their health for money, or a little uncertain present pleasure, and then they would give all they possess to gain back a moiety of it again.

JAMES ROGERS AND OBADIAH ELLSWORTH.

There are two men, James Rogers and Obadiah Ellsworth, living neighbors, who are exactly opposite in their characters and modes of living, and apparently in their views of life—of the use to be made of life, the enjoyment to be derived from it. They both began life poor. They are both lawyers of about equal talent, realizing each an income of about fifteen hundred dollars from his profession, and their necessary expenditures are about equal; that is, they are in the same rank of life, and have families about the same in number.

Obadiah Ellsworth has a wife, two daughters, and a son. His motto is, "Live while you live, and seize the pleasures of the present day;" yet he does not, at the same time, neglect provision for the future. Every day sow some seed, and reap some harvest in the present, is his rule.

He takes journeys, indulges in suitable relaxation when at home, frequents the places of amusement within his reach, enjoys social converse, supplies his table with the luxuries of the season, not extravagantly, but sufficiently for health and enjoyment; provides his literary taste in the same manner, with what is new and desirable in the world of letters, and allows himself time to read it. His hand is open, too, to true charity. With all this the strictest economy is observed in his affairs and his household, as regards any unnecessary waste or extravagant expenditure that will bring little remuneration in true enjoyment. He keeps up this style of living at an expense of about one thousand dollars a year, and lays up five hundred.

Mr. Rogers, the other, reverses this process in every particular. His creed is, give to God each moment as it flies; but his God is Mammon. He allows himself no respite from business, except what is absolutely necessary, in his opinion; not what is requisite, in fact, for the preservation of his health of body, and to preserve the vigor and sprightliness of his faculties of mind. In consequence of this he is less brilliant as a speaker than he would be with the pressure of care and toil occasionally removed from his mind, to give it its true spring; besides, he has several times lost many months from confinement by fever, no doubt induced by overwork; so that he is a direct loser pecuniarily, by his system, if he could but see it, besides the enjoyment of life he misses. His necessary expenses are less, if any thing, than those of his neighbor, Mr. Ellsworth. He, too, has two daughters, who are not generally considered very productive ware; but he has two sons who more than pay their way—so they pour into the family treasury instead of subtracting from it.

These two men have been living upon their present system about twenty years; consequently, Mr. Ellsworth has laid up ten thousand dollars, and enjoyed twenty thousand. He is still hale and vigorous in mind and constitution, promising to be good for business for another twenty years at least, with the same enjoyment in the present, the same provision for the future, for his old age or his children.

. The other has broken health in consequence of over application to business, is nervous—bowed in frame—older than his years. He has not enjoyed the blessings along his daily path—waiting to enjoy much at some future hour, which he will never reach.

CHAPTER XIII.

THOUGHTS AND PERSONS.

THE FACE AND THE THOUGHTS.

If people only knew how a repetition of evil thoughts or unworthy feelings stamps itself upon the countenance in characters not to be mistaken, they would avoid harboring such thoughts, or cherishing such feelings.

I thought thus to-day when I saw Anna Miles. A few years ago she was a bright, smooth, pleasant-faced girl — deceit and evil passions had made no lines upon her face, though their germs were probably in her character. Now it is written all over, crossed and underscored by them. The mouth, especially, shows bitterness—a sneering expression:

"Mouth that marks the envious scorner
With a scorpion in each corner."

THE FACE AND THE THOUGHTS. 247

Every passion and emotion has a handwriting of its own, did we but understand it. Then those who would be beautiful outwardly must cherish noble thoughts and sentiments, elevated feeling, banish pettinesses, if they would not have them reflected in their faces.

We all see or feel the effect that mental and moral culture has upon the face, the movements. How easy to tell the cultured and the uncultured by these! Many would improve interiorly for this, did they fully understand it. If for no higher motive, better this than nothing.

It would be an interesting experiment to take a rude and uncultivated person, yet one susceptible of a high degree of improvement, and subject him to a thorough course of training and development of his threefold nature. It would be curious to note the effect of this process, as every part of his nature was gradually refined, and reduced or increased to its proper proportion.

As the intellect was awakened to watch the dull eye brighten, the brow become clothed with thought, and every feature instinct with the life of mind. To see the countenance lose its gross, heavy-contracted expression, expand and grow symmetrical by the action of the soul, the chiseling of thought; to witness the softening influence of cultivation of the finer sensibilities, modifying not only the tones of the voice, but even the movements of the body, making them more gentle and smooth; to see the uncouth deportment by degrees assume the dignity of self-respect, the ease of self-control, the features would not only become more symmetrical in themselves, by a thorough process of this sort, but the additional luster thrown over them by the light of the noble and truthful qualities brought out in the character, the reflection of moral and intellectual beauty, would render them transcendently lovely.

TRYING TO SEEM YOUNG.

There are some who try to seem younger than they are. There are more who are afraid to appear as young as they really feel. How often we hear elderly people say, when some plan of amusement is afoot, and a proposal is made that they join in it, "I should enjoy it, but how would it look for me to go," or to take part in whatever recreation is proposed! This is wrong. People ought to take part in the innocent amusements of youth, just so long as they can enjoy them. It ought not to be considered indecorous or out of character for them to do so.

How often in a family the older members are laid upon the shelf, when they have lost not one jot of their tastes for the light sports that amuse the younger portion! It seems to be thought a matter of course that they should stay in the background.

Many, from the fear of being suspected of an affectation of youthfulness, run into the other extreme, and endeavor to suppress a native buoyancy of spirit, and keep down the sprightliness of a sportive nature, which, with some persons, remains to extreme age. For this reason they dare not manifest the pleasure they really feel in the sports and amusements of earlier years. We need not voluntarily put away the freshness and joyousness of our hearts, and visages, and manners. The period of their aridness will come soon enough without being anticipated. A good life, which will comprehend a life of strict justice to ourselves and others, not only in great matters, but in the most trivial details, upon which often hang great results, will preserve them in almost perennial youthfulness.

INJUDICIOUS FRIENDS.

I have wondered, sometimes, which would do us most harm, the friendship of some people or their enmity. I am convinced, from observation and experience, that with regard to a certain class the latter is preferable, so far as worldly success is concerned. The tighter they cling to us, the more they are like the "old man of the sea" to Sinbad the Sailor, strangling our efforts and hindering our advancement. Always at sixes and sevens with the world, we can not, if closely connected with them, keep the even tenor of our own way—as one who is linked to the arm of a drunken man can not walk steadily. So these ill-regulated friends, butting against posts, and hitting corners in their intercourse with society, you must in some measure share their mischances.

Do they essay to defend you, it is always in a manner calculated to do you infinitely more harm than good. They will always say the wrong thing at the wrong time, and in the wrong place, setting the conduct they would extenuate in an unfavorable light, instead of palliating it, though actuated by the kindest motives for your welfare. They will repeat something you have said for their ears alone, when it will do you harm, or make you appear absurd and ridiculous—all with the best intentions—having your welfare wholly at heart. If they wish to assist to advance you to any position, they are certain, by the injudicious measures they adopt, to insure your defeat. Better, as I said, an open enemy, than a friend of this description to drag you down, if you are ambitious of worldly distinction. He who uttered this prayer, "Heaven, save me from my friends, I can take care of my enemies," had probably been tried by such a one. You may be assured that he who is not judicious and discriminating in his own matters will not be so in yours; so beware how you trust the reins of your affairs in the hands of another.

INNATE REFINEMENT.

Politeness, good breeding, courtesy, or whatever quality it is that these terms designate, must be innate, instinctive, to be thorough and genuine. A true gentleman or lady must be born, as well as a true poet. To be sure there are forms of manifestations which are to be learned, but the foundation upon which this character rests must be inborn. And we see very little of the genuine article in the market; because, to be truly courteous, one must possess delicate sympathies, and a nice sense of justice, that will prompt due consideration for the feelings and rights of others.

True courtesy requires a good degree of tact, too, of intelligence and refined feeling, that one may always say and do the right thing at the right time, and in a proper manner, so as never to strike an unpleasant chord unnecessarily in those with whom we are associated.

A truly well-bred person will be essentially as polite to the meanest hireling as to a prince, though the manner, of course, will be modified by the different circumstances of the two. "Who causes the fewest persons in a company to feel uneasy, is the best bred," has been said. Who unnecessarily causes uneasiness to others in company, is not well-bred, to be sure; but the converse of this does not always follow; a person may be neutral from sheer stupidity. Or a refined person thrown among the vulgar will cause them to feel uneasy from the very fact of superiority. There is a natural antagonism between refinement and vulgarity; but coarseness, mere want of culture, if the nature be noble, will not render one so repulsive to the truly refined and high-minded, as a low-nature, innate vulgarity glossed over. True courtesy, then, is refined consideration for others gracefully expressed, and requires a combination of qualities seldom met.

To be a perfect gentleman, one must be a perfect man. Has there ever been a true gentleman since Christ left his example for us to follow? Too much ceremony, too rigid an adherence to forms, is a mark of ill-breeding, because they create irksomeness and restraint, and, among persons of the highest refinement, are not necessary, though they must sometimes be used as a defense against the vulgar. There are those so innately coarse and vulgar that they never appreciate any delicate attentions bestowed upon them from courtesy, who never award any preference to others except it is from servility, where they have an object to gain, who know nothing of reciprocity in this matter. Some take all the little preferences shown them as tributes to their superiority, or are, perhaps, so utterly obtuse as to be unconscious that any sacrifice has been made for them by others, or, possibly worse still, they usurp the best privileges, not even leaving to your courtesy the pleasure of bestowing them. With such one is absolutely obliged to lay aside gentleness and consideration in self-defense—though these qualities may be most natural and easy to practice—and meet them in some degree in their own spirit. A person's own good breeding is not always a safeguard against other people's ill-manners.

Many in this, as in other things, present the shadow when the substance is wanting—hang all their goods in the shop window—bear politeness in their superscription, when all is hollow within. No one can be truly polite who does not really feel kindness and consideration for others. And how soon we feel of these empty professions, that there is no heart behind them, like an organ with the false notes ranged in front, nothing behind them to make music!

"Good manners, true, though wrought with finest skill,
Are but the outward garment of good-will."

JUDGE ALDEN, OR THE SELF-MADE MAN IN POWER.

I have been reading to-day an old book, "The Proverbs of all Nations," and a good many thoughts were suggested thereby. Here is one that I have lately seen illustrated: "Now I have got a ewe and a lamb, every one cries, Welcome, Pete!" This was the case with Judge Alden, whose acquaintance I have made recently. The Judge, a few years ago, was a poor student here in the village. Devoting his time to study, earning barely enough to keep soul and body together, he has often, he told me, dined off three cents, eating his meal in a little back room in an old shop, where he boarded himself, lodged, and pursued his studies. He says this way of life was not at all accordant to his natural tastes and inclinations, which were somewhat luxurious; besides, his appetite had been pampered in his younger years by a mother, who was the queen of cooks, and who always provided abundance of the good things of this world for her table.

His parents dying, he and a younger sister were left to their own resources. His sister qualified herself to teach a country school, and he taught occasionally to supply his necessities, pursuing his studies in the mean time. Often, he says, he has envied the prosperous citizens when seeing them going home to a comfortable dinner. But, with one or two exceptions, it did not seem to occur to these same well-to-do citizens to invite the poor student to partake of a dinner with them, though they had enough and to spare—though he was a genial companion, possessing a fund of intelligence, and a view of genuine wit and humor, and conversational powers suited to give these free play when their flow was excited by good cheer, and a sense that his society was appreciated.

Now, many of these men, blessed with good dinners, were not correspondingly blessed with intelligence and an aptitude for conversation that would enliven the social board, having their minds mostly occupied by turning a penny to the best advantage, and he might with propriety have said to them what, with a little variation, a poor humorist once said to the wealthy patrons whose tables he was wont to enliven by his sallies, "You have money—good dinners—which *I* want, and I have wit which *you* want." And with equal propriety might they, if appealed to in his behalf, have replied as one of their class is said to have done to an appeal for assistance to a poor but worthy young man, "Why should I promote merit? merit never promoted me."

But to return to the Judge and his dinners. There was a widow lady in the neighborhood, who was not blessed with an abundance of this world's goods, but who had sons near the young man's age that valued him, who used occasionally to send him a present of a mince pie, or a bunch of sausages, or some bread, or fruit, and permitted her sons sometimes to invite him home to dinner or tea. He told me he should never forget how he enjoyed her plain meals, which were epicurean feasts compared with his usual meager fare. Then there were two more families in the village, in moderate circumstances, having sons, who used once in a while to invite him. He was universally well spoken of in the village as a young man of studious, industrious habits, and of unexceptionable morals, and undoubtedly possessing talent, but he had not come to his broadcloth yet; slept hard and fared hard in his little back room; and so our substantial citizens, many of whom had themselves risen from small beginnings, forgetting, that of such material many of our presidents and statesmen have been made, gave no heed to the young student toiling in his cheerless room.

How easily might they, by encouraging his efforts, and manifesting an interest in them, and rendering occasionally some trifling aid, even in the way of a dinner, have smoothed his way, strengthened and cheered his endeavors, and secured to themselves what their mere gold could not buy—the gratitude of a generous heart!

Well, after completing his law studies, he went

West in search of that success and appreciation of his talents which a rising young man is more apt to meet elsewhere than in *his own country*. He did rise, quite rapidly too, not as light bodies mount, but by force of peculiar merit. His name appeared in the papers of the region where he lived, coupled with the epithets "gentlemanly," "talented," etc., in notices of public meetings, political and otherwise, where he had acted a conspicuous part. Then news came that by a fortunate hit in land speculation, or some keen foresight, wealth had come to him, not vast, but enough to add weight to his position, and increase his influence, and future fortunate speculations in the same line were spoken of as probable.

At the end of six years he made his appearance again in the village whence he had gone forth a penniless, coarsely-clad young man, whose existence among them had scarcely been recognized by the more prosperous inhabitants of said village. Now, he came with the prestige of popularity, and acknowledged worth and talent, from his adopted western home. He made his advent, clad in broadcloth, and in place of the old fur cap, so distasteful to eyes polite—albeit there were good brains beneath it—was a shining beaver, a much better letter of introduction, inasmuch as there are more who can judge of the quality of a beaver than of those who can discern the quality or quantity of brains a man hath.

What obsequious bows, what cordial grasps of the hand he met from those who but a little time before had passed him coldly, unheedingly by! What invitations to dinner, breakfast, and tea flowed in upon him, where he had often been dinnerless and supperless for want of wherewithal to supply these meals! Now, when he possessed the means to gratify his most luxurious tastes in these particulars, how solicitous every one seemed to minister to his gratification in them! Horses and equipages were placed at his disposal, now that he was able to hire them; before, he would have trudged on foot a long distance, or lacked a refreshing ride a long time, and it never would have entered the head of one of these persons to offer him one, illustrating another proverb—I do n't remember it exactly—about, "if a man has a horse he can borrow, and if he has none he may trudge afoot," or something to that effect.

Young ladies who would have scouted any attentions from him, when he used to perambulate their streets in the dilapidated fur cap and suit of "hodden gray," seemed proud now to receive any gallantry from him; and mammas, who would once almost have driven him from their doors with a broomstick, had he offered to call on their daughters, showed now an anxiety to smooth the way for all these gallantries. Though this was not a new phase of human nature to him, its exhibition struck him forcibly with its lamentable and ludicrous features when shown so glaringly in his own case.

It is quite probable that some feeling of contempt toward these assiduous persons, who were so eager to bestow favors upon him, mingled with his appreciation of their efforts in that direction.

But though these things did not open up to him any new vista in his view of human nature, something that met him in another quarter surprised and perplexed him; yet it was, in reality, as easy of explanation as the phenomena that had appeared upon the other side, though referable, perhaps, to a more praiseworthy principle in human nature.

This that puzzled and hurt him was the shyness, coldness, and reserve manifested toward him by those from whom, in his less prosperous days, he had received kindness and sympathy in his struggles to gain an education and a position among men. His heart warmed with gratitude as he recalled the kind offices bestowed by these few upon the poor student, from whom they could expect nothing in return, and which were of priceless value to him in the bare state of his affairs, as a crust to one starving may prove of higher worth than the greatest luxury in the midst of abundance. The highest pleasure he had anticipated from visiting former scenes was, that he might greet again those who had shown that they possessed genuine, friendly, humane, benevolent feelings, unalloyed by selfishness; but when they met him so coldly, his own feelings were chilled, and he did not, at first, understand it. The solution of the matter was, that he had come back elevated so far above these, his former associates, in wealth, position, and the splendor of his outward appointments, that they were doubtful as to how far he would recognize them, judging from almost universal precedent, which taught them that people generally *shed* those friends for whom they have no further use.

Two or three had bestowed favors upon him, elicited by his needs alone; the occasion for this was past, and they met him with indifference, not saying by their manner, "do you remember what I did for you once?" They saw, too—all these persons—that he was courted by a class that looked down upon them—and they were not certain that he had sufficient true manliness of character to recognize them fully and cordially in opposition to this fact, and, as I said before, almost universal precedent, and they threw themselves upon their independence and reserved rights till they should ascertain how the opposite party would comport himself.

CHAPTER XIV.

MY JOTTINGS ENDED.

DISAGREEABLE PEOPLE.

If we do not "cultivate a taste for disagreeable people," as a facetious writer has recommended, it is at least necessary that we cultivate toleration of their presence and forbearance toward them, for it is unavoidable that we should meet them at every turn of our progress through life; that is, those whose views, feelings, tastes, and pursuits may be diametrically opposed to, or uncongenial with ours. A neglect to acquire this spirit will strew our path with thorns and nettles that will be continually wounding or annoying us.

Perhaps we women—especially women of our class—from the peculiarity of our position, are more frequently subjected to annoyances arising from the presence of persons not agreeable to us.

Men have business, outside duties, that take them away from disagreeable guests, while it is our business to entertain them. Very tiresome it is sometimes; but I am not certain that we always bear these things with the equanimity we ought, or that we do not suffer them to mar our enjoyment much more than is necessary. We must meet these people at home and abroad, that is inevitable. Who has not had an anticipated pleasant visit spoiled by the presence of some other guest that was distasteful?

For instance, you go on a visit to your particular friend Mrs. Sykes, expecting to enjoy yourself vastly, talking over old times, and taking little drives and walks with her. When you arrive you find Miss Blount, also a friend of your hostess, already a guest, established for the season. Miss Blount is not altogether agreeable to you. On the contrary, she is somewhat the reverse; she interrupts your little confidential tête-à-têtes, with which she has nothing in common. On your return from a visit you check your comments upon persons and things which you are accustomed to make freely to your friend, and somehow you feel her presence a restraint upon your spontaneity of thought and feeling.

Your code of politeness tells you that you should treat with consideration guests met at the house of a friend, even if they should be such as would not be welcomed at your own, so you try to conceal your distaste for her, but you are illy successful. Miss Blount appears no more easy in your society than you in hers; you are probably as much of an interruption to her pleasure as she to yours; but this you do not consider. Miss Blount is really a very worthy person in her way, as you are forced to acknowledge. She is correct in her habits and deportment, so far as you can see; still you sympathize with the sentiment of the quatrain:

> "I do not like thee, Dr. Fell;
> The reason why I can not tell:
> But this fact do I know full well,
> That I do n't like thee, Dr. Fell."

You are going to ride with an agreeable friend, and expect to derive much pleasure from observations upon scenery, and an exchange of remarks upon persons and things met by the way, which you have before enjoyed upon similar occasions. While you are indulging in these pleasant anticipations, your friend drives up, accompanied by his cousin Matilda, who has come on a visit, and must not be neglected. The barometer of your expectation falls suddenly several degrees. You try to look gratified by this unexpected addition to your party, but your smile of welcome looks more like a twinge of the toothache. Were cousin Matilda at all intuitive—which fortunately for her she is not—she would discover she was *de trop*, and be constrained accordingly; but in blissful unconsciousness of this fact, she is the freest and merriest of the party; you feel that your spirits have all gone over to her, and a resentful feeling rises, as though she had robbed you of a property in the landscape, and the conversation of her cousin.

That persons are not particularly pleasing to us is not always to be taken as proof positive of want of merit in them. In many cases it may be exactly the reverse. An article of food may be perfectly unexceptionable in itself, and pleasing to some tastes, yet not suit other palates. The unpalatable dish may be set aside, or refused without blame. The persons who are distasteful to us can not be so easily disposed of. What is to be done? Why, accept them as unavoidable when they fall in our way, and try to make the best of them. Endeavor to cultivate toward them the spirit of Uncle Toby—"the world is wide enough for thee and me"—and remember that this same world, and the things in it, were constructed for the convenience of several individuals besides yourself, who have an undoubted right to their use.

A little philosophy of this sort will tend wonderfully to reduce many of our annoyances from the source of which I have been speaking, and, mixed with the oil of resignation to whatever is unavoidable, will help to remove "friction from the wheels of life."

> Human foresight to the wisest
> Leaves them oft but choice of ill;
> Though thou well-set schemes devisest,
> 'T will not always work thy will.

BENEFIT OF WRITING.

Many are afraid of *wasting time* in mental improvement—giving to it time that ought to be devoted to something else. There is little danger of this. It does not often occur, though we often read of women who reverse the true order of things in this. They are much more likely to neglect their duties for frivolity—something that is for show alone. But I was going to speak of the benefit of jotting down a thought or two of our own or others each day, and how much matter would accumulate in this way in a short time. Only five lines a day, which I can accomplish in five minutes, would make quite a respectable volume—in size—in the course of five years.

For the six months that I have been boarding here, having more leisure to write, as well as more time for observation and reflection, I have averaged about one page per day. I could have done much more, only I thought I must get a great deal of sewing done, so I could keep leisure to write when I went to housekeeping again. Perhaps this is as much as would have been profitable; besides, I wanted to give a good deal of time to reading, to discipline and correct my thoughts and language. I expect to increase this amount for the rest of the time, for it becomes constantly easier for me to write; and by the end of the year, if I do so, I shall have quite a book, if the *quality* would only bear a proportion to the bulk, which is not certain. I shall not always have so good an opportunity for writing and study, nor so many helps and suggestors to thought as I have here; so I must try to improve my privileges, for I do not know where we may go next.

HENRY MAYBERRY'S WEDDING.

I have been to Henry's wedding. I never saw any thing so lovely as Sarah looked when she stood up during the ceremony. I could well imagine that of such are the angels. Her illness, her suffering, have so etherealized her, and now her countenance was overspread with a divine radiance of joy, tempered with a gentle modesty, that made her loveliness almost superhuman.

They were married in the morning at eight; we had breakfast at nine, and set off on our journey about ten. The step-mother was very gracious, and nothing had been omitted in the necessary arrangements for the occasion. Indeed, the matter was rather overdone. The breakfast-table was literally loaded with an abundance and variety of food. I heard one old lady guest remark, "It is n't every step-mother would take so much pains—I know that!"

I thought, if as much labor and expense as have been given to the getting up of this feast had been expended in good offices for Sarah during her illness, how her feelings might have been soothed by the sympathy evinced, or that seemed to be evinced.

POPPING CORN.

"What shall I write about?" I asked of Maggie, as she sat in the corner.

"Take a kernel of corn," she said, bestowing a handful in the popper, and shaking it over the coals.

In a minute it was converted into a snowy mass, ten times its former bulk, beautiful to the eye as well as delicious to the taste.

"Would it not seem like magic," I said, "to one unacquainted with the nature of the process, to see these insignificant-looking grains burst suddenly forth into beautiful white blossoms? Would it not excite the wonder of the king of Siam as much as the fact that water could be made to become solid rock, which he did not believe?"

How many beautiful and wonderful things pass under our eyes every day, but which custom has so familiarized we give them no heed! The most beautiful and curious phenomena scarcely excite in us an emotion of pleasure or a feeling of wonder. We go groping with our half-closed eyes fixed in the dust at our feet, when we might feast them with glory and beauty. The sublime panorama of the sky, to a mind attuned aright, would be ever pleasing, ever new. And what delight the variety which earth presents might afford us, in its Summer carpet of green, begemmed with a countless variety of flowers; or in Winter's robe of spotless white, sometimes by the jeweler Sun bestrewn with countless gems of the most gorgeous and delicate dyes, the diamond, the opal, and all precious stones!

And not only do we neglect what is pleasing in our daily life, but we do not set a sufficient value upon our substantial blessings. Instead of trying to make the most of them by a process analogous to popping the corn, expanding and beautifying them, and by a mental alchemy transmuting even evils to blessings, like the bees of Trebizond, gathering honey from poisonous flowers, we reverse the process, sucking poison from the fairest. We look at our privileges through the little end of the telescope, making them appear small and distant, while we hug and magnify our disadvantages, rolling all that is bitter and unpleasant in our pathway like a sweet morsel under our tongues.

THE SELFISH.

The worst of it is with selfish persons, they never know they are selfish. This is the most incurable symptom in their case; if they yield a little to others, they have no idea but that they cover the whole ground. They do not know how often they trample upon the rights and privileges of those about them, because they never think of them; and not to think of others, which is sometimes made an excuse by the selfish, is the very essence of all selfishness. They do not know that they expose themselves by the very refuge behind which they attempt to hide.

Another distinguishing feature of selfish persons is, that they accept the sacrifices of others, without knowing that any have been made for them, so completely absorbed are they by self. By these marks they may be known.

KINDNESS TO ANIMALS.

Little things indicate character. Walking out the other day beyond the limits of the village, I came to a nice-looking farm-house. I will stop and rest a little, I said to myself, and get a draught of water, "sparkling with coolness," from that well in the yard; so I opened the gate and went in.

A large, well-kept-looking dog lay, sentinel-like, on the front door-stone. I shrank at first, but as he looked at me with an eye a little curious, but kindly, I addressed him by an imaginary name, at which he came down from his perch, wagging me a welcome, and trotted along patronizingly by my side, without a bark or a growl, showing himself not only well fed, but well bred, quite different from the dogs at a house I had passed a little while before, where "Tray, Blanche, and Sweetheart," all ran out and barked furiously at me.

As I passed around I saw pots of flowers sitting in the porch. Things promise well here, I said to myself, though cultivation of flowers is not to be taken as unfailing evidence of refinement of taste. It often results from imitation, as well as an innate love of the beautiful, as with fine clothes, fine houses, fine pictures, and fine furniture, people have them because their neighbors have them. We have seen a child sitting on the floor muttering over a piece of paper or a book, in imitation of his father, who is enjoying a literary feast, reading some favorite author. He does not know but that he has the same enjoyment from his book or paper as his father from his. So these imitators do not know but their birds and flowers, and the objects of beauty they have gathered around them, afford them as fine and exquisite a pleasure as is derived from them by those of cultivated tastes.

Rapping at the door, a neat and pleasant-looking lady presented herself, who, I saw at once, was the mistress of the house. She invited me to step in, and I did so, taking the nicely-stuffed chair she proffered me. Though not approving of stuffed chairs, on general principles, I found this very comfortable. I made myself known, and then fell into conversation with the lady upon the weather, the appearance of the neighborhood, etc. Glancing around, I saw behind the stove a couple of chairs, each chair having a cushion in it, and on each cushion a sleek, plump cat, looking so placid, and so enjoying the sense of existence, with their heads resting on their velvety paws, that it soothed me to look at them. My mind referred back to the well-kept-looking dog I had seen, and I glanced involuntarily at the mistress of these comfortable animals to see if her bump of benevolence was not well developed.

It was. Then a sound of music came to me—not an instrument, but bird music—poured forth from melodious throats. Raising my eyes, there, before and above me, hung two capacious bird-cages, and in each, on their perches, two glossy-plumaged canaries, singing thus their thanks to their mistress, as well as their Maker, for the happiness they enjoyed. The cage was clean and well supplied with bird luxuries; and though I always feel a sense of pain at seeing a bird in bondage, even though it is made tolerable by kind care and attention, these birds seemed happy. The woman was not aware that by all these things I was gauging her character. She had acted from the impulses of a kindly nature, making the dumb creatures dependent on her comfortable; but I had seen contrasting cases—dogs and cats meager looking, skulking, in momentary expectation of a blow; dirty, close cages, crowded with ragged-plumaged canaries, too depressed to pipe a note. How I have longed to open the cage door and set these miserable prisoners free!

There is a doctrine that all the animals one abuses in this life will have a chance to retaliate in another. If this be true, what torments must be endured by some owners of cats, dogs, and horses! What lashings and starvings, what kicks and cuffs, and pinchings with cold and hunger, are in store for them!

FAREWELL.

And now, kind reader, we must take our leave. These jottings have given occupation to many an hour that otherwise would have been idle, listless, and wearisome. They have called back the sunny as well as the sad memories of the past—days when I was younger and stronger than now. I know not as I have been guided by any plan or special purpose—only to jot down thoughts and incidents. Whether they would ever be read by another; or, if read, whether they would possess any special charm, or convey any suggestive influence, has entered little into my thoughts. All I can claim for them is that they are pictures from life. The most I can hope for them now is, that they may beguile the weary hour of some toiler in the vineyard, bring cheer to some sorrowing heart, disclose footprints of experience that may prove a useful guide to the bewildered, and also strengthen for toil and triumph the Christian laborer. If the reader shall wish to know of my present, it may satisfy him that sunshine still falls upon my path.

www.ingramcontent.com/pod-product-compliance
Lightning Source LLC
Chambersburg PA
CBHW032122230426
43672CB00009B/1832